ANGLIA • PREFECT • POPULAR

ANGLIA • PREFECT • POPULAR

From Ford Eight to 105E

MICHAEL ALLEN

MRP

MOTOR RACING PUBLICATIONS LTD
Unit 6, The Pilton Estate, 46 Pitlake, Croydon CR0 3RY, England

ISBN 0 947981 07 1
First published 1986

Photosetting by Zee Creative Ltd, London SW16
Printed in Great Britain by Netherwood, Dalton & Co. Ltd, Bradley Mills, Huddersfield, West Yorkshire

Contents

Foreword

by Fred Hart

Fred Hart joined the Ford Motor Company in 1940 as a draughtsman working on armoured fighting vehicles and other armaments. He qualified in mechanical engineering during the war. After some years as staff engineer involved in the design of cars including the Mk 1 Zephyrs he was made Executive Engineer Light Cars and was responsible for the engineering of the 105E Anglia. He followed this success with the Cortina Mk 1 and Mk 2, each of these models selling over one million cars. After other model successes he became Chief Engineer Cars for Ford in 1963. He left the company in 1969 to become Technical Director at GKN, finally retiring in 1979.

I am grateful to the author of this splendid, detailed history of Ford small cars over the last 50 years for it enabled me, as the responsible engineer for part of that history, to stand back and review not only the successes of the period but to analyse any detail failures that occurred as a result of inadequate engineering or compromise.

In a worldwide market which is the target for all Ford cars, compromise is the inevitable result of satisfying the conditions demanded by terrain, climate, legislation, drive side, preference etc, and of course, competitive practice. A successful model can only emerge after painstaking attention to every market requirement.

To be the best and stay there requires every facility and expertise that can be provided, and so, shortly after the war, Ford engineering had the competitive advantage of having their own test track where prototype cars were subjected to every kind of ride, handling, durability and component stressing that was required by market conditions. In addition, adequate numbers of prototypes were scheduled for testing and development in differing world terrains and climates.

Racing and rallying does improve the breed and the setting up of a competitions department at the time of the 100E's introduction had an influence on the products that followed, with engines, suspensions and drive trains benefiting. This influence was especially advantageous when we engineered the Cortina GT, one of the most successful cars ever to be produced by Ford.

I commend this excellent book for its interesting presentation and for the accuracy of its detail.

F. L. Hart

Acknowledgements

Three generations of Ford Anglias, and the other homely little Fords derived from them, hold fond memories for very many people. These models, more than any others, were the way Ford of Britain realized Henry Ford's dream of providing thoroughly dependable motor cars for the masses at the lowest possible prices. They grew to be part of daily life and their names became household words. I can still remember waiting eagerly at the front-room window one teatime in the summer of 1951, ready to catch the first glimpse of the new Anglia which my father was collecting that day, our first postwar car; and then, a few years later, the thrill of getting my own first car, a 2-year-old 100E Anglia. It has been particularly pleasing, therefore, to write this history of the small Dagenham Fords, and here I wish to acknowledge the many people who have helped so willingly with the supply of information, literature and photographs. In particular my thanks go to David Burgess-Wise, of Ford Motor Company Public Affairs, for the material he made available, and his excellent hospitality when I visited Brentwood; Steve Clark, Sheila Knapman, and all the staff of Ford Photographic at South Ockendon; former Ford engineers Les Geary, George Halford and Fred Hart, the latter who, having been closely associated with the birth of the 105E Anglia, kindly offered to write a foreword to this book; fellow author, and acknowledged sidevalve-Ford expert, Dave Turner, for making available many photographs, Martin Howard, and Steve Waldenberg, another well-known sidevalve-Ford enthusiast and hard-working member of the Ford Sidevalve Owners' Club; founder 105E Club member Paul Guinness, and co-founder John Colyer, who loaned me much material from his 105E collection, as did Keith Roe and Keith Trotter. Thanks are also due to Marcus Pye, of *Autosport*, Ray Hutton, formerly of *Autocar* and John Thorpe, of *Motor*, for their kind permission to use performance figures and quotes from the road-test reports which have appeared in their respective magazines. Anglias have figured prominently in various forms of motor sport, and in this respect I am very grateful to Anne Hall, Jeff Uren, Maurice Gatsonides and Edward Harrison for their time when answering queries, and for the loan of photographs from their collections; thanks also go to Alan Mann, and former works drivers Nancy Mitchell, Gerry Burgess, Jack Reece and Norman Quick, also to Mark Doughty for information on the Montlhéry record-breaking Anglia. For information in respect of their present-day competition Anglias I am grateful to Kevin Owen, Simon Bridge, Tom Luff and Martin Collins; with particular thanks to Archie Inglis for the most enjoyable (from the passenger seat) demonstration of his Anglia's capabilities, and to David Dunlop and Frank Hall for the photos of Archie's car. Thanks, too, to Pauline Bradley, Harold English, David Chiltern, John Slocombe and photographer John Allen, for their help in setting up the jacket photo-session. Finally, to MRP's John Blunsden, for giving me the opportunity to write the Anglia story.

January 1986   Michael G. D. Allen

CHAPTER 1

Ford at Dagenham

The need for a small car

Henry Ford's 'Detroit of Europe', the magnificent purpose-built motor manufacturing complex by the side of the river Thames at Dagenham, Essex, was officially opened in October 1931. With its own docking facilities and railway link, its own power station, foundry and advanced assembly lines, the Dagenham plant was indeed the most modern and best equipped outside the United States. Its workforce — soon to be swelled by many who were already employed at the company's Trafford Park, Manchester, assembly plant, and who with their families and entire belongings were to be transported in specially chartered company trains and rehoused at Dagenham — were to enjoy excellent working conditions. A 40-hour, five-day week was coupled with high wage rates, subsidized hot meals were distributed to strategic parts of the factory at lunchtime on heated trolleys, and the workers' hot and cold washing and cleaning facilities were complete with showers.

There was, however, one very serious problem. The Ford Motor Company simply did not have a suitable car to build for the British and European markets. The famous Model T had enjoyed considerable success in Britain in its early years, but it had been hit hard by the horsepower rating method of road taxation introduced in Britain in 1920. This tax, in which the nominal horsepower was calculated on the bore size only rather than on the total capacity of the engine, was not only heavily biased against the large-bore Ford engine with its 20hp rating, but was destined to stifle engine development in Britain for almost 30 years, its absurd method of calculation forcing designers to retain very narrow bore diameters.

Production of the legendary Model T had finally ceased in 1927 after more than 15 million examples had been sold worldwide. The replacement model which appeared later in the year was so advanced by comparison that Henry Ford felt entirely justified in starting the 'alphabet' series all over again, and so the new car emerged as the Model A. The Model A's engine, with a capacity of 3.2 litres, had a 24hp rating, but as a grudging concession to the ludicrous horsepower tax in Britain there was to be a small-bore version, reduced in size to 2 litres and with a 14.9hp rating, for assembly at Trafford Park and to be known as the Model AF. However, whilst the Model A proved to be another international success, with more than 5 million produced in its 4-year production run, the Model AF derivative was a

The Model Y, here taking part in an early sales campaign, was the first Ford designed specifically for Europe in general and Britain in particular. Price cuts in 1935 made possible the famous announcement of the '£100 Ford'.

dismal failure in Britain. What in fact had been needed in that market, of course, was not just a lower-powered version of a comparatively large car, but a genuine economy model which would not only satisfy the demands of those who were purchasing cars like the Austin Seven, but would also if possible bring new-car ownership within the reach of even lower income groups.

Henry Ford appears to have been well aware of the situation, for in 1928 he had had drawings prepared for a direct competitor to the Austin Seven, although, rather surprisingly, the company's staff in England had not been particularly enthusiastic; apparently the thinking at that time was that the Model AF would gradually re-establish Ford fortunes in Britain. In the event, however, it did not, and in 1930 some 15 examples of small British and other European cars crossed the Atlantic for evaluation by the Ford chiefs in Dearborn with a view to drawing up plans for a competitive product.

Meanwhile, construction work at the Dagenham site was going smoothly. Henry's son, Edsel, had turned the first turf there at a ceremony the previous year, thus setting in motion a sequence of events which were now quickly transforming 600 acres of Essex marshland into a mighty motor manufacturing industrial estate that would include the premises of Briggs Motor Bodies and the Kelsey Hayes Wheel Company in addition to Ford themselves. During 1931, as work at Dagenham was nearing

An early production Model Y saloon. The spare wheel was mounted vertically at the rear and no luggage boot was provided but a small grid could accommodate a suitcase externally.

A longer radiator grille, with the front bumper appropriately restyled, and valanced front wings characterized later Model Ys. The chrome lamps and screen surround, twin wipers and trafficators indicate that this four-door is a De Luxe model.

completion, the already poor sales performance of the Model AF took a downward turn, and by the time the plant opened in October the request from Ford of Britain for a small car to build had assumed a rather desperate tone.

Henry Ford now ordered work to begin on a prototype 8hp model, and by December a neat little car, hiding behind 'Mercury' badges, was to be seen running around Dearborn. In February 1932 this car was exhibited by Ford at the Albert Hall, in London, whilst similar prototypes were being shown elsewhere in countries where Ford had an interest. Known at this stage as the Model 19E, the new car was viewed enthusiastically by dealers and public alike, and plans to mass-produce a similar car at Dagenham quickly took shape, with the result that in August the company was able to offer the public the first 8hp Ford.

The production models — now designated Model Y — displayed some differences from the prototypes. Rather more rake-back was applied to the radiator cowl and the windscreen, which, with the flowing wing design and the 17in diameter welded-spoke wire wheels, resulted in a very elegantly

Miss Finland 1934 shows off a Model 40 V8 Ford which, though it post-dated the Model Y, reveals the strong American connection in the smaller car's body design, the style perhaps lent more flair by the larger scale. Not until later were British Fords allowed to develop a cut of their own.

styled car indeed by the small-car standards of the day. The bodywork was also 2in wider than that of the prototype thus ensuring ample, rather than just adequate room for four persons. Devoid of both water pump and oil filter, the new sidevalve engine nevertheless featured a crankshaft running in three main bearings — a notable mechanical refinement not to be found elsewhere at that time amongst small economy models. A bore diameter of 56.6mm resulted in a 7.96hp rating, and a stroke of 92.5mm gave a total capacity of 933cc. Mated to the engine was a new three-speed gearbox, its ratios being selected by a long direct-acting floor-mounted lever. Synchromesh between the upper two ratios was another refinement making an early appearance on an economy car. There was the usual Ford torque-tube drive to a spiral-bevel rear axle assembly, and the simple chassis also featured the established Ford suspension arrangements consisting of transverse leaf springs at both front and rear.

Priced at £120 and £135 for the two and four-door models, respectively, the new Ford offered far more in terms of performance, refinement and accommodation than similarly priced rivals such as the Austin Seven and Morris Minor, and Ford of Britain's popularity started a rapid climb. Detail changes kept the Model Y more than competitive, but it was faced with a very serious rival late in 1934 with the announcement of the new Morris 8. As is now well-known, Morris had purchased a Model Y Ford and studied it very carefully indeed, with the result that their new car was markedly similar in many respects whilst actually having the advantage of rather more sophisticated running gear, including hydraulic brakes. Ford countered with a series of price-cuts, culminating in the announcement of the £100 Ford Popular in October 1935, at which time the basic Morris was £120.

At about the same time as the Morris 8 appeared, the Model Y had been joined in production at Dagenham by a 10hp stablemate — the Model C — and so Ford were still extremely well-placed to satisfy the demands of many of those at the lower end of the market. Although sharing the same wheelbase — 7ft 6in — as the 8hp car, the Model C was built on a different chassis of more rigid construction, which was also wider in the middle in order to accommodate a more roomy body, again available in both two and four-door configuration. The Model C's styling carried more than just a hint of the company's V8 models. Being scaled down drastically by comparison with the larger cars, yet still quite broad in the middle for its size, this model earned nicknames such as 'Barrel Billy' and 'The Sugarloaf Ford'. Under the bonnet, of course, was a larger-capacity engine — the now legendary 1,172cc Ford Ten. A new cylinder block, which could nevertheless be machined on the same tooling as the 8hp unit, allowed a bore size of 63.5mm, whilst the piston stroke remained the same 92.5mm as on the smaller engine. Available only as a De Luxe model, and priced at £135 (two-door) and £145 (four-door), to which £5 had to be added if leather upholstery was specified, with a further £5 for a sliding roof, the Model C Ford was soon generally accepted to be offering the best value in the 10hp class.

The 8hp and 10hp Fords inevitably attracted a wide following, not just because of the remarkable value they represented, but also because of performance characteristics which were usually sufficient to put them clearly ahead of their most obvious rivals on the road, thus making them a particularly attractive proposition for the 'sporting' driver with a limited

The 10hp Model C Ford was available only in De Luxe guise. Later cars, recognizable by the horizontal bars on the radiator grille, as shown here, were designated CX. The number plate looks as much of an afterthought as it did on the Model Y.

The pretty 10hp Tourer, with cutaway doors and a windscreen considerably different from that of the saloon version.

purse. The performance aspect was often stressed in the motoring press, and comments which appeared in *The Autocar* during 1936 clearly underline the superiority in terms of speed and acceleration which the small Fords possessed. Testing the basic £100 Popular, *The Autocar* said of its performance: '... as acquaintance with this car is gained, it is soon realized that not only does it give motoring in an economical and easily attained form, but that actually it performs exceedingly well as a car with an 8hp engine.... As anyone can see who follows performance — and that of small cars in particular — the figures in the table show up well. Indeed, there is an inclination to suggest that for this car to be capable of as much as 62mph as was achieved at Brooklands with the assistance of a favourable wind, is more than necessary... the acceleration and climbing abilities belong almost to a larger category of vehicle, due to a lively engine and low total weight.' The little car had accelerated from rest to 50mph in 34.4 seconds, and covered the 20-to-40mph range in 18.6 seconds in top gear and in a very creditable 12.2 seconds in its useful middle ratio.

With an unladen weight of 16cwt, the four-door Model C was 2cwt heavier than the two-door and rather slimmer-bodied Model Y tested, but the 1,172cc engine more than made up for this, and here again *The Autocar* were rich in praise for the car's performance, commenting: 'There is achievement represented on a manufacturer's part when it is possible to say of each model produced that it provides exceptional performance, particularly where acceleration is concerned. This is undeniably the case with the various Ford models. Especially is the performance of the Ford V8 noted for its briskness, and one is inclined, in reviewing the 10hp car, to go as far as to say that among small cars other than those of sports type this possesses a "V8 performance". It is remarkably lively on the road, being pleasing and untiring to handle as a small car largely for the reason that it does so much for its size and, incidentally, for its price. It is full of life, and meets the driver's ideas of what he wants in acceleration and cruising speed.... The pick-up on top gear, even from quite low speeds, is extremely good, so that many a larger car is matched by this Ford's performance... an exceptionally good getaway from rest can be made, again out of proportion to what might be expected from a 10hp car.... At 50 the engine is still not fussy, while, as the test figures show, it is capable of propelling the car at a speed approaching 70mph.' The figures recorded were a mean maximum speed of 65.4mph, with a best one-way speed of 68.1mph, and acceleration from rest to 50 and 60mph in 22.6 and 39 seconds, whilst fuel consumption was said to be 32-35mpg. The car tested, late in 1936, was complete with all the options at £155, and *The Autocar* concluded: 'Undoubtedly, as a car capable of carrying four people comfortably, interesting to drive, yet economical to run, the De Luxe Ford is outstanding value.' Praise such as this must have been gratifying indeed to the Ford Motor Company, and few would have been surprised if the 8hp and 10hp models had continued unchanged for some years ahead. In fact, both cars were nearing the end of their production run, as work on the projected replacement models, which in turn would quickly evolve into the first of the Anglias and Prefects, was now well advanced.

CHAPTER 2

Anglia, Prefect and Popular

The famous upright Fords

In 1935, looking to the future, and considering eventual replacements for the successful Y and C type cars, Dagenham took the bold step of designing and building prototypes themselves. Bold, because participation in design by anybody outside Dearborn was, to say the least, discouraged by the parent company. It is said that when, late in 1935, young Dagenham executive Patrick Hennessey (later Sir Patrick Hennessey, Chairman of the company) arrived in Dearborn with two prototypes, he was 'thrown out' by Charles (Cast Iron Charlie) Sorensen, Henry Ford's righthand man for many years. However, Dearborn relented soon after, and Dagenham was given the go-ahead to develop the new cars, which were to be known as the Eight and Ten.

Two new chassis were decided upon, both having channel-section longitudinal members, inverted U-section transverse members, and rear seat and luggage space platform of similar construction to those of the superseded Model C, but the Ten now featuring a longer — 7ft 10in — wheelbase. The suspension arrangements followed the earlier pattern, but with the transverse leaf springs now mounted ahead of the axle at the front and well behind at the rear, thus lengthening the spring base with a beneficial effect on ride and handling qualities, whilst a flatter rear spring than previously resulted in improved roll resistance. As before, Burman worm-and-nut steering gear was employed. Mechanically-operated brakes were also retained, but with improvements incorporated to transmit more pressure to the trailing shoes.

The engines were virtually unchanged, although a bypass oil filter could now be specified. On the Ten the gearbox was also as before, but on the Eight lower first and second ratios were adopted in order to provide similar initial acceleration and hill-climbing abilities to the superseded Model Y, despite a heavier body, both cars now weighing in at about the same as the preceding 10hp model. The torque-tube drive and spiral-bevel rear axle assembly, with a ratio of 5.5:1, was similar, although rather stronger than previously. In both cases the wheels were now of the easy-clean pressed-steel disc type; in addition to being cheaper to produce, they also looked far more appropriate on the new cars, which had lost the rather 'spindly' look of their predecessors.

The Ford Ten — designated 7W — appeared first, in March 1937, and was available with both two and four-door bodywork which bore no

resemblance at all to the earlier cars. All the doors were now hinged at their forward edge, a useful safety feature which also ensured easy entry to and exit from a passenger compartment of very ample proportions for four people. The longer wheelbase had allowed the rear seat to be mounted slightly ahead of the axle line, with a consequent improvement in riding qualities, whilst still giving usefully more legroom than before. Cloth upholstery was standard, with real leather once again being available as an extra-cost option, as was a sliding roof. Sun visors, twin vacuum-operated windscreen wipers, self-cancelling flush-fitting trafficators, winding windows in the doors and an opening windscreen were all standard features. At the rear, access to the luggage compartment was via an external drop-down lid with adjustable straps which would allow it to be secured at any angle. A separate compartment beneath this, with its own external access, housed the spare wheel in a horizontal position. With prices of £143 (two-door) and £150 (four-door) being only £8 and £5 above those of the preceding Model C, the new Ten offered outstanding all-round value amongst small saloons, whilst for those who appreciated open-car motoring there was also available at £150 an attractive two-door Tourer with a weatherproof folding hood.

Production of the short-wheelbase Eight, the 7Y, began in August 1937, just 5 years after the first 8hp Ford had appeared. Now produced solely as a two-door car, the new 7Y closely resembled its 10hp stablemate, being distinguished at the front only by its radiator grille with a single rather than triple aperture. At the rear, the Eight was easily recognizable with its spare

16

wheel housed upright in a recess in the flat back panel, uncovered on the basic model, but concealed by a circular steel cover on the De Luxe. Inside, there was slightly less room in the rear compartment due to the retention of the shorter wheelbase, although access via the very wide doors and fold-forward front seat squabs was relatively easy, and certainly more dignified than with the rear-hinged doors of the earlier car. The basic model, with Rexine upholstery and a rather spartan equipment level, was sold for £117 10s. A further £10 would purchase the De Luxe model with additional features such as an ammeter, electric clock, trafficators (self-cancelling), twin wipers, interior light, cloth upholstery, chrome-plated hubcaps and windscreen surround — a specification very similar to the 10hp car. However, £10 was a sizeable sum in the 1930s, and the basic model outsold the De Luxe, although, interestingly, production records indicate that some 300 buyers of the basic car were nevertheless willing to pay the £5 extra demanded for a sliding sunshine roof.

Styling changes to the Ten were introduced in October 1938, these consisting principally of a new, rather more upright radiator grille and a single-piece rear-hinged bonnet top. A useful innovation was the provision of a vacuum reservoir in the wiper system, enabling the wipers to keep going somewhat longer when the accelerator was fully open. The wipers themselves were now scuttle-mounted. With these changes came the designation E93A and the name Prefect — making it the first Ford car to bear a model name. A very elegant two-door drophead coupe, complete with outside frame irons, replaced the earlier Tourer. Leather upholstery was standard on this version, which offered rather more closed-car snugness with its hood raised than had the previous model. Priced at £185, the coupe was pitched rather more up-market than the saloons.

This view of the E93A Prefect shows the fabric centre roof section which was a standard feature of Dagenham bodywork prior to the adoption of monocoque construction.

Restyling of the Eight did not take place until late the following year, and in fact the Second World War was into its third month when the E04A Anglia was announced in November 1939. A rather plain and very upright radiator was a prominent feature, although, unlike on the Prefect, the lengthened bonnet retained the centre-hinged side-opening arrangement. At the rear, an added-on boot with a similar dropdown lid to that of the Prefect was a welcome addition from both a convenience and a styling viewpoint, giving the car a better visual balance when viewed from the side. The basic model, available only in blue or black, and recognizable externally by its black-painted wheels and hubcaps, fixed windscreen with a rubber surround and lack of running-boards, was now £126, with a further £10 being asked once again for the comprehensively equipped De Luxe car.

The Autocar tested a De Luxe Anglia early in 1940, publishing their findings in the issue of April 26 and, as usual, the performance came in for praise with the comment: 'Total weight is almost exactly the same as the previous model (7Y), and the performance remains of the lively order which has been associated with the 8hp Ford throughout its history. The four-cylinder sidevalve engine is a hard and willing worker, but also smooth and very reasonably quiet over the greater part of its speed range. Second gear can be used freely to give "snap" to the acceleration and hill-climbing, but in spite of the modest size of the engine there is good top gear power and, in general, no impression of it being necessary to resort over-frequently to the gearbox.' The Anglia, in fact, had proved to be capable of almost exactly 60mph and accelerated from rest to 50mph in 35.4 seconds, this being accompanied by a fuel consumption average of around 44mpg. Other comments included: 'Exceptional luggage space is afforded for a car of this size.... The general interior finish is pleasingly done. Equipment includes a rear window blind conveniently operated from the driving seat, a sun visor for the driver, and built-in ashtrays.... Twin suction-operated wipers sweep practically the whole width of the glass, and there is the valuable point of a reservoir device which overcomes the natural habit of vacuum-operated wipers to stop working temporarily when the throttle is opened wide... and [the wipers] have the further pleasing point that when put out of action by the control the blades automatically "park" themselves out of sight.'

Production continued during 1940, and a prototype Anglia version of the two-door coupe was built with the intention of exhibiting it at the 1940 Earls Court Motor Show. In the event, however, with the worsening wartime situation, the show was cancelled, by which time Fords for public consumption had in any case ceased to leave the Dagenham factory. The resources of the Ford Motor Company were now needed to produce rather more warlike equipment than Anglias and Prefects, although some cars were built for ministry and service use, and the well-known E83W semi-forward-control 10hp van, which utilized many Anglia and Prefect components, was produced for a variety of wartime roles.

Postwar production began in June 1945, with just one model each of the Anglia and Prefect, these being effectively an amalgamation of the previous basic and De Luxe specifications. Twin wipers were fitted, but on the Anglia the windscreen was fixed and with just the plain rubber surround. Running-boards were also absent from the Anglia's specification. A major improvement was the adoption of 10in diameter brake drums in place of the previous 8in front/7in rear diameters: now with 85sq in of brake lining area, the small Fords had excellent stopping power.

The 933cc 8hp engine of the E04A Anglia. The Model Y engine, the first of the line, had a crankshaft without counterbalance weights, but with the arrival of the 10hp unit in 1934 came a counterbalanced shaft which was applicable to both engines.

In addition there were a host of minor improvements, these including a cartridge-type oil filter, moisture-proof ignition leads, anti-condensation plug caps and a longer-lasting silencer. Changes on the Prefect only were a larger generator and larger-section tyres. As the new 5.00-section tyres were mounted on smaller-diameter — 16in — rims, the Prefect was now pulling slightly lower overall gearing (13.5mph/1000rpm) than the Anglia (13.8mph/1000rpm), which retained the 4.50 x 17 tyre/rim combination. An interior light and a rear window blind continued to be features of the Prefect only, and both cars were available now with just black or white paintwork.

Relatively few of these early postwar cars were to be seen on the roads of Britain, as this was a period when exporting was vital the nation's recovery after the devastating years of war, and as two of the qualities then inherent in anything bearing the name Ford were ruggedness and serviceability, the Anglia and Prefect were enjoying worldwide success. Export models differed in several respects, with two-door Prefects still being available in certain countries, as were 10hp Anglias with the prewar-style 7W-type grille.

A popular feature of the motoring magazines were the road test reports which appeared regularly in their pages, but rather different from these was a very interesting 'off road' test conducted by *The Motor* in 1947. The car used was an Anglia, and it was chosen because at £293 (wartime inflation and the imposition of purchase tax having more than doubled car prices) it was the cheapest car available in Britain. The route chosen was the

Peacetime again, and a rather more spartan Anglia went back into production, almost devoid of chrome and without running-boards.

For 1949 the Anglia acquired 'new' frontal treatment which was, in fact, almost the same as that of the 1937 cars. The model was now designated E494A.

Alongside the 1949 Anglia came the E493A Prefect, complete with restyled 'modern' front end, the headlamps now set into much deeper front wings.

Ridgeway, a 55-mile track dating back to pre-Roman days, extending westwards from the Thames Valley, and paved only for very short stretches where it coincided with the modern road network. Despite the fact that one of the objectives was 'to see just how much punishment a popular British saloon will stand', the Ford Motor Company did not hesitate to provide a car for the trip, supplying not a brand new example, but a company 'hack' with 22,000 miles on the clock. The Anglia completed the westward trip inside a day, some of the uphill sections being taken with tyre pressures down to 15psi and two of the three-man crew riding on the rear bumper. The crew were so impressed with the car's ability that they decided to make a similar return journey using other cross-country tracks wherever possible, including the disused Harrow Way. Summing up this interesting two-day excursion, *The Motor* stated: 'There is nothing impassable about the Harrow Way, but the disused sections are rough and overgrown. In a last despairing effort to do the poor Ford a bit of no good, we stormed the ruts diagonally and fast, but in vain. It may well be that the transverse springing, which frankly allows the car to sway somewhat at high speeds on cambered roads, gives useful lateral cushioning at times, but certainly ill-treatment which should have produced buckled wheels left the car entirely unmoved. For two full days we had been as cruel as possible to the Anglia, over some of the worst tracks of southern England. We had tackled every sort of hazard, steep gradients, mud, water, ruts and hard bumpy surfaces, and the car at the end of the trip was filthy, but as quiet, lively and controllable as at the start.'

Meanwhile, an example of the cheapest 10hp car in Britain, the Prefect, now at £352, was being subjected to the more normal road-test procedure

The last of the long line of 'upright' Fords was the 103E Popular, its Anglia-style two-door body totally devoid of unnecessary trim, with silver-painted bumpers and, of course, no running-boards.

by *The Autocar*, the report appearing in the issue of January 23, 1948. Pointing out 'this is, by a very appreciable margin, the lowest-priced 10hp-rated car at present on the British market', *The Autocar* went on: 'It proves a speedy form of transport, when required, with the ability to hold around 50mph — one cannot say quietly, but very stoutly and with not the slightest indication that all is not well …. The engine is noisy, chiefly with the sound of induction roar, under acceleration and at full power, but, as already indicated, perfectly happy…. In point of fact there is little more noise at 60 than at 50mph, and it was found that in the favourable direction of the wind the Prefect would run up to a genuine speed of as much as 68mph…. Average speed capabilities on a journey are decidedly good, and in the course of a few days spent trying the car under varying conditions, one arrives at a very real respect for the Prefect's obviously rugged qualities.' Of the suspension, it was said 'it gives comfortable riding in the sense that it takes the shock very well indeed out of poor surfaces…. There is, however, roll on corners if fairly enterprising methods are indulged in, and some pitching occurs over less good surfaces.'

October 1948 saw the introduction of facelifted models with the designations E494A Anglia and E493A Prefect. In both cases it was the frontal treatment which came in for revision, with the Anglia now reverting to a version of the nicely raked-back prewar 7Y/7W-type grille, twin apertures replacing the earlier single or triple arrangement. A new grille, bearing a marked resemblance to that of the V8 Pilot, was now a feature of the Prefect, which in addition received new front wings incorporating flush-fitting built-in headlamps in the modern fashion — these lamps also being more powerful than before. Inside, the Prefect now sported an elegant sprung steering wheel, which was also to be found on export Anglias. Delicate shades of green and fawn were now added to the range of colours available.

These modifications could not, of course, conceal the fact that the small Fords were still very much 1930s cars, and in view of postwar developments

The facia and controls of the Popular. The radio fitted to this example was an extra-cost option, but the ammeter and winding windows were standard features despite the rock-bottom price.

from rival manufacturers there was surprise now in some quarters that nothing genuinely new had appeared from Dagenham, as the recently introduced V8 Pilot was also only a mildly restyled version of the prewar V8 model. However, technically outdated as they were, particularly so in respect of the suspension arrangements, the Anglia and Prefect were nevertheless very comprehensively equipped by the accepted small-car standards of the period. They displayed a high standard of workmanship and finish, had excellent performance coupled to good overall economy, well-proven durability, and offered new-car ownership at unbeatable prices. By continuing to produce what was effectively their prewar range at prices which alone ensured their continued success, Dagenham were buying valuable time during which to develop their new medium/large range intended to cover both the important $1\frac{1}{2}$-litre category and that for high-performance saloons. This new range was eventually to appear in October 1950 as the then revolutionary Consul and Zephyr Six, the former

As a boy, working on his father's farm, Henry Ford dreamed of producing mechanical means of replacing the horse and easing the farm labourer's burden. That particular dream was not realized until 1917, when the first Fordson tractor went into production, some time after the Model T had given substance to his other vision of producing a car 'for the great multitude'. That those two aims continued to be fulfilled is shown in this picture, taken some years after Ford's death, of a new Ford Popular — the cheapest car in the world — with the finest farm tractor of its time, the Fordson Major.

filling a noticeable gap in the Ford range whilst the latter would take over at the top from the ageing V8 Pilot — and it was only then that serious development on new economy models could take place.

Meanwhile, the 8hp and 10hp Fords, with their established reputation for economic dependability, continued to make new friends. Petrol rationing was still quite severe in the early postwar years, and in 1950 an interesting conversion aimed at eking out the precious fluid became available for the Anglia. A new inlet manifold retained the standard Zenith carburettor, outboard of which was an additional similar Zenith instrument fed from an auxiliary tank containing methanol. A progressive accelerator linkage ensured that the car started and ran at low speeds/light throttle openings on petrol, with the methanol being introduced at around 35mph cruising speed, but from lower speeds during wide-throttle acceleration. Open-road cruising was claimed to give about 40mpg on a 50/50 mixture of the two fuels, thus allowing considerable more mileage to be obtained from the basic petrol ration. The conversion was developed by the Island Garage, in Birmingham, and quite a few cars in that locality were converted. The E494A and E493A models continued unchanged until deleted in October 1953, at which time they were replaced by the completely new 100E Anglia and Prefect.

But this was not to be the end of this small-Ford line which already spanned 21 years. The E494A had retained its position as the least expensive car available in Britain, being priced at the end at £445. The new 100E Anglia, however, at £511, was being undercut by the Austin A30 (£475) and the new Standard Eight (£481), and so there was room now for a basic bottom-of-the-range new car. This appeared on October 21, 1953 as the Ford Popular 103E, at the bargain price of £390. Apart from the fact that it was powered by the 10hp engine, the Popular was in effect a detrimmed and appreciably less well-equipped version of the preceding Anglia model.

Externally, chrome-plating was now almost non-existent, being confined to the door handles and the thin trim strips around the grille openings. The bumpers, now silver-painted, were without overriders and the hubcaps

A late model 103E Popular shows off its frontal aspect. That twin-aperture grille has more than an echo of BMW about it – or did Ford do it first?

Tail-end treatment of the 'World's Best Motoring Value'. The number-plate bracket, complete with lamp, was hinged so that the boot lid could be left open, secured in the horizontal position by straps, to form an extra luggage platform.

were painted in the body colour. Smaller headlamps were fitted, and the single windscreen wiper, without the benefit of a vacuum reservoir, was mounted above the screen in prewar fashion. No sunvisors were provided, and even trafficators were only available as an extra-cost option. The instrument panel was in plain painted steel, but did include an ammeter in addition to the essential speedometer and fuel contents gauge. A few early models sported the expensive-looking three-spoked sprung steering wheel from the old Prefect — presumably unused stocks — but these soon gave way to a simple two-spoked wheel. Window winders were retained in both doors, but the door trims and seat coverings were rather plainer in style. The upholstery was in the durable PVC which had taken over from Rexine some time previously at Dagenham, whilst the floor was covered in a PVC-coated felt. No parcel tray was provided under the facia, and neither were there ashtrays or an interior light, although these latter items were available at extra cost. A carriage key sufficed to open the luggage boot, which itself was actually slightly roomier now due to the omission of the previous false floor above the spare wheel.

Basic though it was, the Popular offered new-car motoring not just for some 20% less than the cheapest opposition, but at more than £50 less than the preceding Anglia. It was in every way a 'real' car — indeed, its top gear performance between 15 and 55mph was better than some $1\frac{1}{2}$-litre models at that time, a fact that would give many owners of this humble Ford a considerable amount of satisfaction on the road, and it is no surprise that it gained a wide following. In less than two years, production of the 103E Popular reached 85,000 and, as Dagenham was almost 'bursting at the seams', production of the car was transferred to the former Briggs Motor Bodies plant at Doncaster (Ford had bought the Briggs concern two years earlier to give them total control over their own body supplies). The last Popular left the line at Dagenham on July 21, 1955, and during the ensuing fortnight, which was the company's annual holiday time, the entire assembly facilities and body stamping dies for the Popular were moved to Doncaster in a massive £180,000 operation, the first car leaving the line there on August 8. In order to maintain continuity of the high standard of workmanship demanded in the final assembly operations, key personnel recruited in Doncaster had been on special courses at Dagenham, and were now accompanied at Doncaster by experienced men temporarily on loan from Dagenham to assist in getting production smoothly under way.

The Popular continued to be made for another 4 years, during which time only minimal changes occurred in the car's basic specification, such as the adoption of safety glass in 1956 and the fitting of the 100E Anglia steering wheel late in 1957. Production ended in August 1959, with the 103E model having finally added 155,000 cars to the previous half-million 'upright' Ford saloons.

CHAPTER 3

A new generation

100E: progress at last

Following the introduction of the company's new Consul and Zephyr models, production of which had begun early in 1951, small-Ford enthusiasts eagerly awaited news of a new Anglia/Prefect range. Early thoughts on the subject at Dagenham were to have two quite distinct new small cars, the cheaper of which would have been very spartan indeed in order to ensure that it would be yet again the cheapest car available, despite having to absorb development costs. However, as we have seen, a more attractive solution to that problem was to continue the old-type Anglia in a somewhat detrimmed form as the new Popular when the time came, and so remove any restrictions which might have been necessary in the development of the new range simply to ensure a rock-bottom selling price.

Once again, the Anglia and Prefect would be two and four-door cars, respectively, and with differing trim and equipment levels, but otherwise based on identical bodyshells of monocoque construction. The styling was to follow closely that of the successful Consul/Zephyr range, although the new bodyshells were not actually scaled-down versions of the larger Dagenham cars, instead having been designed from scratch around the smaller dimensions necessary.

A very substantial scuttle/bulkhead structure protruded forward at either side to include the top mounting points for the independent front suspension units, these being of the MacPherson strut type pioneered so successfully on the Consul/Zephyr cars. The welded-up floorpan was reinforced by longitudinal inverted U-section members which at the front provided engine mounting points and the forward locating points of the transverse anti-roll bar, and at the rear the fore-and-aft mountings of the longitudinal semi-elliptic leaf springs. Three similar U-section members were welded in transversly, two under the passenger compartment and one above the rear axle, whilst aiding rigidity at the front of the car was another welded-in bulkhead with apertures for the radiator and headlamp bowls. Detachable front wings and an outer front panel containing the grille completed the front end, whilst the outer rear wings and rather high back panel formed part of the integral construction.

A 7-gallon fuel tank resided in the nearside of the full-width luggage compartment, with the spare wheel situated horizontally on the floor to the offside. Despite these intrusions, the capacity for luggage was considerable

The new 100E Ford, here in Anglia form, represented a dramatic leap forward in appearance from the essentially prewar styling of its immediate forerunners.

by previous small-Ford standards, and the provision of a counterbalanced lid made for easier loading over the high back panel. At the front, the front-hinged and very wide bonnet top was also self-supporting, and gave generally good access to those parts needing routine attention. Access to the rear seats on the two-door model was via the passenger side only, where the front seat was arranged to tip forward. The rear seat was placed slightly ahead of the axle line in the interests of riding comfort, and in this position it still allowed adequate legroom, for although the wheelbase — 7ft 3in — was shorter than on the old models, this was due to the fact that the independent front suspension allowed the front axle line to be moved rearwards. Window-winding mechanism was a feature of the front doors, with fixed rear quarter-windows on the Anglia and balanced drop windows in the Prefect's rear doors.

Upholstery in PVC differed slightly in pattern between the two cars, the interior trim being completed with a cloth rooflining and fully-fitted moulded rubber floor coverings. A large full-width parcel shelf ran beneath a simple facia, and the instruments — three circular dials in the Anglia, and a stylized arc-shaped speedometer incorporating the fuel gauge and ammeter in the Prefect — were housed in a binnacle around the steering column. On the centre boss of the simple two-spoked steering wheel was the self-cancelling switch for the flashing indicators, and on the Anglia a recessed horn button, whereas the Prefect's steering wheel was adorned by an elegant half horn ring. Despite the adoption of a 12-volt electrical system for the first time on a small Ford, the time-honoured suction-operated wipers, albeit with a vacuum reservoir, were retained. A single wiper and just one sunvisor were economies to be found on the Anglia only.

Externally, too, the Anglia was the plainer of the two cars, its three painted grille bars and the bumpers being relieved only by thin chromium centre strips, whilst its front and rear screen surrounds were in plain rubber. In contrast, the four-door car displayed considerably more brightwork, including a chromed grille surround, fully chromed bumpers, headlamp

A relative lack of ornamentation left the Anglia's frontal aspect pleasingly clean and simple. The styling was obviously Consul/ Zephyr-derived, but by no means simply a scaled-down version of the larger car.

Rear view is equally uncluttered. The rear window was appreciably larger than those of most other small saloons at the time. A carriage key was provided to open the boot.

hoods and inserts in the screen rubbers. Both cars had plated door handles, whilst the chromed hubcaps were borrowed straight from the Consul/Zephyr models.

Mention has already been made of the suspension arrangements, the MacPherson struts of course incorporating the telescopic dampers and being embraced by coil springs. Damping at the rear was also by telescopic units, angled so that their upper attachment points were both forward and inward of their bottom locations on the rear axle. The Burman steering gear followed the Consul/Zephyr layout with the worm-and-peg steering box situated behind the front axle line and controlling the direction of the front wheels via a three-piece track rod arrangement. The Girling all-hydraulic braking system featured 7in diameter drums and a total lining area which, at 67.2sq in, seemed marginal on cars with an unladen weight in excess of 15cwt and a 70mph speed potential. A 5.20 x 13 tyre-and-rim combination completed the very up-to-date running gear.

Under the bonnet of both cars, to the surprise of many people, was a sidevalve engine with bore and stroke measurements identical to those of the old 10hp cars, although, in fact, it was a completely new unit. It was no secret that Dagenham were very enthusiastic about overhead valve layouts and an oversquare bore/stroke ratio, these features having been successfully combined in the Consul/Zephyr engines, and most observers had naturally expected similar, although smaller-capacity units in the new small Fords. However, considerable sums of money had been spent on the creation of the completely new Consul/Zephyr range, and economies were desirable if possible in the introduction of the new small cars. By designing a new sidevalve engine around the existing bore centres and bore/stroke measurements, much existing production machinery could be utilized, thus offering worthwhile savings in the overall development costs.

The new cylinder block featured larger inlet ports, larger main bearings, and cooling arrangements which included water ducts to the exhaust valve seatings and an impeller-type pump as an integral part of the system. The cast alloy steel crankshaft had larger-diameter bearing surfaces and improved counterbalancing, which promised smoother running at high rpm. The new connecting rods and bearing caps, however, still featured cast-in white metal bearing surfaces, as on the earlier engines, although these could now be machined-out to accept replaceable shells if required during reconditioning. Adjustable tappets were a useful improvement from the servicing point of view.

Neat styling touches such as the flattened wheel arch shapes and the straight-through waistline contrived to give the 100E a surprisingly long look for what was in fact a very compact car. This Prefect shows the swivelling quarter-lights and repositioned wing ornament introduced early in production.

The larger inlet valves, a Solex carburettor and a new cylinder head of 7.0:1 compression ratio (6.1:1 on the earlier engine) were responsible for a 20% increase in nett bhp to 36 at 4,500rpm (30bhp at 4,000 on the earlier engine), and as maximum torque was up from 46lb/ft to 54lb/ft excellent all-round performance was promised. The new engine in fact shared no components with the older 10hp unit, which continued in the 103E Popular, nor was there any interchangeability between it and the uprated 1,172cc unit which had appeared in the 1952 German Ford Taunus 12M, there being no organized liaison in those days between Dagenham and Cologne.

The clutch was operated hydraulically by a similar pendant pedal to that of the braking system, and the power was once again transmitted through a three-speed gearbox. Synchromesh was provided between the two upper ratios but, unfortunately, was not available on bottom gear: the middle ratio was deliberately low enough to allow its use down to a crawl, so virtually eliminating the need to engage first gear on the move, but limiting the value of second as an overtaking gear. Behind the gearbox now was an open propeller shaft, as the new rear axle locating arrangements obviated

31

the need for torque-tube drive. A spiral-bevel final-drive assembly had a ratio of 4.429:1, this giving slightly higher overall gearing than before at 14.8mph/1,000rpm.

Announced in late September 1953, both the Anglia and Prefect were on show at Earls Court the following month. With prices of £511 and £560 they were pitched straight into what was becoming a hotly contested market sector: in addition to the well-established Austin A30 (£504) and the Morris Minor at £529 and £574 in two and four-door configuration, there was the new Standard Eight, a four-door car with a rather spartan trim level, which was nevertheless an attractive proposition at £481. All of these cars were lighter than the new Fords and had OHV engines, although of only 803cc in each case, and as their four-speed gearboxes had relatively low indirect ratios, their third-gear potential was little more than the 100E's second-gear maximum. In terms of speed and acceleration this translated into obvious superiority on the part of the new Fords, but they would not be able to match the really excellent fuel economy which the smaller, but very efficient, OHV engines in the rival cars offered.

Production of the 100E began late in October, with only Anglias at first leaving the line, these eventually being joined by Prefects in mid-December. Meanwhile, prototypes built exactly to production standards were made available to the motoring press, and *The Motor* published a full report of a Prefect in their issue of December 9, 1953, commenting: 'If cars

Close-up of the massive scuttle/ bulkhead structure of the 100E: this was only Dagenham's second monocoque body, the first being the Mk 1 Consul/ Zephyr. Like the Consul/Zephyr shell, the 100E's was over-engineered to an almost amazing extent in the light of what later proved possible, as no chances were taken with strength at a time when the cars had to sell in markets where unmade roads were common.

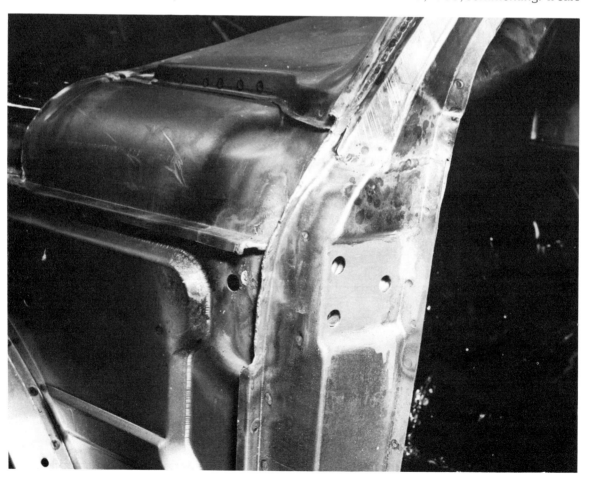

assembled on the production line are as attractive as the Ford Prefect which we have recently driven for a very substantial mileage, a car which had been built by hand but which conformed precisely to the finally agreed specification, then the production models which are due to appear will be in very great demand.' By comparison with the previous model it was noted: 'In performance it has rather less top gear "snap" below 40mph, but much more above that speed, acceleration through the gears being much improved and the maximum speed going up by almost 10mph. Whereas the old Prefect was rugged rather than refined, however, this latest model offers exceptionally good springing, and has cornering power which approaches the standards expected of sports cars, as well as being quieter and much smarter in appearance.' The new 1,172cc engine was said to have 'surprised us pleasantly by operating happily on standard rather than premium grades of petrol.' Also in respect of the engine it was thought: 'The flexibility is entirely satisfactory by four-cylinder standards, low-speed smoothness only being spoiled by "waggle" of the central gear-lever at speeds below 12mph in top gear, and at the opposite end of the scale it is only above 60mph that the power unit becomes at all conspicuous.' Of the three-speed gearbox it was noted: 'Inevitably, very slow traffic does sometimes call for the engagement of the non-synchromesh first gear with the car on the move, while the more sporting drivers may long for an "overtaking" ratio which would be useful up to more than 40-45mph, but the excellent new three-speed gearbox is a happy compromise which most purchasers will fully approve.' Summing up, *The Motor* felt that '... the Ford Prefect offers things which no other car (except the similar Ford Anglia two-

The forward protrusions of the bulkhead structure to accommodate the tops of the front suspension struts are clearly evident in this underbonnet view. The bonnet lid is hinged at its forward edge and assumes a vertical position when open, giving good access from the side on what is a relatively narrow car, though restricting it from the front.

THERMOSTAT
VALVE
PISTON
PISTON RINGS
PISTON PIN
WATER PUMP IMPELLOR
FAN
WATER PUMP
VALVE GUIDE
VALVE SPRING
VALVE SPRING RETAINER
VALVE COTTERS
CONNECTING ROD
VALVE ADJUSTER
VALVE TAPPET
TIMING SPROCKETS
CRANKSHAFT PULLEY
TIMING CHAIN
CRANKSHAFT
FILTER SCREEN

DISTRIBUTOR
CARBURETTOR
SPARK PLUG
INLET MANIFOLD
COUNTER WEIGHT
EXHAUST MANIFOLD
SPRING
EXHAUST CONTROL VALVE
VENTILATION PIPE
OIL PRESSURE WARNING LIGHT SWITCH
PRESSURE PLATE
MAIN BEARING LINER
CLUTCH DISC
THRUST WASHER
FUEL PUMP
STARTER RING GEAR
SUMP
OIL PUMP
OIL RELIEF VALVE

Cutaway view of the 100E engine. The sidevalve layout and the coolant passages around the valves can be seen, as can the crankshaft counter-weights. Readily apparent differences from the earlier Eight and Ten engines are the adjustable tappets and the provision of a water pump and thermostat in the cooling system.

door saloon) offers at the same price. With four seats of adequate if not especially generous roominess, it combines speed, economy, comfort of riding and good cornering qualities in a manner which should earn it a huge circle of friends.' These comments were echoed some time later when *The Motor* reported on a production Anglia, summing up this time: 'In all, this new Anglia is a worthy addition to the Ford range, offering, at the cost of perhaps rather less economy of fuel, considerably more performance than do any other cars of comparable price, and so combining with its utilitarian virtues a large measure of appeal to the enthusiast.' Both cars had recorded almost identical performance and economy figures, with an ability to exceed 70mph very slightly and reach 60mph from rest in 30 seconds being accompanied by fuel consumption in the 30 to 40mpg range. As well as selling in very large numbers indeed, the new Fords were quickly to be seen in competitive events, and this prompted *Autosport* to take a look at the Anglia, with John Bolster reporting his findings in the issue of August 13, 1954.

'Some readers may be surprised,' he started, 'when they learn the subject of this week's road test. It is quite true that normal family saloons seldom figure in *Autosport's* pages.... Yet the latest small Ford has another side to its character, and one that renders it of considerable interest even to the sporting motorist. It was the rally drivers who first discovered the potentialities of this car. They brought back tales of phenomenal average speeds over difficult terrain.... This they said was something new in small cars...' After briefly describing the various features, he continued: 'When

Three separate dials and the lack of a horn-ring identify this as an Anglia facia. The contemporary Prefect had a crescent-shaped speedometer in an otherwise similar instrument binnacle.

The restyled facia which appeared late in 1955 with the introduction of the De Luxe saloons is seen here on a Squire estate car.

the engine is idling a fair amount of vibration is transmitted to the body. As soon as the revolutions mount, however, the unit proves to be far smoother and quieter than the original "1172". Naturally, the enthusiast would prefer a four-speed gearbox, but second speed gives rapid acceleration up to 45mph, and is a useful traffic gear.... In two respects, the Anglia is better than any other small British saloon. The first of these is the absence of road and tyre noise.... The Anglia scores very high marks for a quiet interior, and all my passengers remarked on this feature. The other respect in which the Ford excels is fast cornering. The roadholding and general controllability set a new standard for this class of car. It is possible to enter sharp corners at 60 or 70mph and to take them with an effortless ease that is simply uncanny.... I must admit that I drove the car very hard all the while I had it,

The long gearlever came conveniently close to the steering wheel rim and provided a direct, quick-acting change when required.

for the engine seems perfectly happy to cruise at nearly its maximum speed. If one were content to travel at more reasonable velocities, I am sure the petrol consumption would average at least 35mpg.' In Bolster's hands the Anglia had accelerated from rest to 50 and 60mph in 15.4 and 26 seconds, reached a true two-way average of 72mph and returned 30mpg. He concluded: 'A few years ago small family saloons were slow, stodgy, and unpleasant to drive. Today, many of them handle as well as a good sports car, and they can keep up an average that would not disgrace that type of vehicle. The new Ford Anglia is one of the best of the bunch, and it is backed by the worldwide service of the parent organization. At £511 2s 6d it is, to say the least, quite a proposition.'

Clearly, the Anglia and Prefect were already offering high standards of performance and roadability for this class of car and at the prices asked they represented all-round value which was very much in the Ford tradition.

Nevertheless, the cars on display at Earls Court in October 1954 featured minor improvements. The Anglia now had a lockable handle rather than the carriage key at first provided to open the boot, twin wipers with plated arms, door straps, an interior lamp, and chromed inserts for the windscreen and rear window surround. Both front seats could now be tipped forward. In both cars, the rear seat backrest had a different rake, there was now a footrest alongside the accelerator pedal and ashtrays made an appearance in the rear compartment. The Prefect's rear doors now had the benefit of winding windows.

When reporting on the Anglia and Prefect, *The Motor* had mentioned the fact that the brakes could be made to smoke and judder under extremely hard use, although actual fade had apparently only been slight. Improvements introduced in January 1955 consisted of 8in diameter

37

The trim and equipment of the Escort version of the estate car approximated to those of the Anglia De luxe saloon.

At the rear, a convenient horizontally-split tailgate was provided for loading this useful little vehicle.

drums housing shoes with a lining area of 76.8sq in, these dimensions being much more in keeping with the car's performance capabilities. Another change early in 1955 was in answer to criticism from some drivers concerning the fact that the unsynchronized first gear sometimes had to be engaged whilst on the move. Slightly lower indirect ratios were introduced: first gear was now almost relegated to being a starting ratio only, whilst second gear had lost some 3 or 4mph of its usefulness at the top end, and to the enthusiastic driver this was a retrograde step.

One way of modifying these ratios was to fit the HandA overdrive unit offered as an extra for the 100E by H and A Engineering Ltd. It was intended principally as an economy device, but it did offer the enthusiast a much wider choice of ratios as it could be engaged in any gear — including

reverse! Unlike the more sophisticated devices from Borg-Warner and Laycock used on some other cars, the HandA featured unsynchronized dog clutch engagement, which produced a slight 'clatter' when changing in or out, and had a vacuum-operated change mechanism which required the driver to push the control in for a full second whilst also disengaging the clutch — a rather ponderous arrangement. Used on second gear it did provide faster acceleration than top up to about 55mph, and so could provide a useful overtaking ratio in some circumstances. Considered as an economy device, it offered substantial improvements in the 40 to 60mph range where an extra 6 or 7mpg could be obtained. However, with a price of £40 10s plus a fitting charge of about £5, it would only offer worthwhile savings for the high-mileage long-distance business user. On the 19.9mph/1,000rpm overall gearing which the HandA provided, the sidevalve engine would barely pull 3,500rpm, so maximum speed was not improved.

The 100E range was expanded considerably in October 1955 with the introduction of both De Luxe versions of the saloons and estate car derivatives. Recognizable externally by a full-length chrome side moulding, chromed door window surrounds, twin wing mirrors and, for the first time in the case of the Anglia, chromed bumpers, the De Luxe saloons also featured much improved interiors with two-tone trim combinations. A new facia panel housed two circular instruments and improved switchgear that did away with the earlier lighting switch with its curious three-position — sidelamps on/everything off/headlamps on — arrangement. Redesigned front seat squabs actually gave more rear compartment kneeroom. Twin sunvisors were provided, as were twin horns, but the Prefect unfortunately lost its elegant horn ring, both cars having a central button which operated one horn with a gentle push or both with greater pressure. The difference between the De Luxe and basic cars was made more marked by the deletion of some of the previous standard fittings from the basic models, these now having painted wiper arms and being without the chrome screen surround inserts, whilst inside the interior light was deleted. The basic prices were unchanged, and the De Luxe models seemed decidely the better value at £542 and £596 for the Anglia and Prefect respectively. The two estate cars were the Escort, which, where appropriate, corresponded

Sliding side windows were another Squire feature. The timber strips, a faint echo of the old 'woody' style, persisted until the October 1957 facelift when they were deleted, as shown by the left-hand-drive car above.

40

externally to the Anglia, and the Squire, which matched the Prefect. Both were trimmed and equipped to the De Luxe standards, and at £587 and £631 were priced a little higher than the equivalent saloons. Stiffer rear springs, lever-arm shock absorbers, and larger-section tyres — 5.60 x 13 — were fitted, the latter raising the overall gearing very slightly, but the gearbox had lower indirect ratios than those of the saloon to ensure easy starting in the fully laden condition.

The crisp styling of these small Fords had been very well received from the start, and in October 1957, four years after the model had first appeared, only mild external changes were considered necessary to keep the 100E in the forefront of small-car fashion. A useful revision at this time was an appreciably larger rear screen, which was now an instant recognition feature from behind, as were new rear lamp clusters. A new, simple mesh grille, chromed on the De luxe version, was introduced for the Anglia. Both cars now had painted head and sidelamp surrounds, but with chromed inserts on the De Luxe models. Full-length chrome side strips still identified the De Luxe cars, but the wing mirrors were deleted from the

A larger rear screen and new rear light clusters were prominent amongst the restyling details for the saloons in October 1957.

The facelift included a new grille for the Anglia version. The flattened V-shaped bonnet motif appeared on both cars, replacing the Anglia's simple strip and the Prefect's 'Aeroplane' device. UWW 447 was photographed in daily use some years ago.

A post-facelift Anglia displays the additional brightwork – windscreen surround and side trim strip – of the De Luxe version, as well as the fashionable contemporary option of whitewall tyres.

42

The Anglia interior from October 1957 onwards. De Luxe cars had a lockable glove compartment in place of the parcel shelf seen on the standard model, above.

specification. A completely new facia characterized the interior, with twin circular dials once more, but these were now mounted either side of the steering column. The wide parcel shelf remained a feature of the basic models, its place on the De Luxe cars now being taken by a lockable compartment. A pale-coloured vinyl roof lining combined with the new larger rear window to give a lighter effect to the interior scene.

The mechanical specification remained unchanged, although an interesting new option — two-pedal control — was available. The system used was the Newton and Bennett 'Newtondrive', in which a centrifugally-operated clutch was disengaged at idling speeds, but automatically took up the drive from rest as engine revolutions increased. For gearchanging when on the move the centrifugal arrangement was overriden, the clutch being disengaged by a normal withdrawal lever connected to a vacuum servo, this being activated by depressing a switch in the gearlever knob. The choke control and accelerator pedal were connected to operate another overriding mechanism which caused the clutch to remain disengaged at

44

Control layout of a 107E Prefect, much the same as the previous, sidevalve-engined car, but with the gearlever, now operating a four-speed box, further aft on the central tunnel.

fast idling speeds with the choke in use, but to engage as soon as the accelerator was depressed. Pushing in the choke control returned the system to the normal centrifugal mode.

An Anglia De Luxe equipped with this system was tested by *The Autocar*, the report appearing in the issue of May 9, 1958. Comment on the two-pedal system, which cost £24 extra, was not particularly favourable: 'Concentration is required to move the car gently from rest, even with a warm engine, and the right foot on the throttle pedal must be controlled almost as delicately as the left on the clutch pedal of a conventional transmission. Manoeuvring — especially in reverse — on the gravel surface of many a private drive becomes, indeed, quite a skilled and potentially embarrassing operation, the more so when any gradient is involved.... Yet on the car tested the actual clutch take-up was reasonably smooth.... For a downward change from top to second — a very wide gap in ratios — the engine speed had to be gauged very accurately to avoid a jerk, for the clutch cannot be engaged progressively — it is either *in* or *out*.' In other respects, of course, the Anglia's behaviour was as before, with the handling and braking earning such comments as: 'This Ford is an excellent manifestation of the advances made in small-car design in recent years. Even cars which are built to compete in the lowest price categories now can often claim qualities of steering, braking, suspension and roadholding equal to those of much more expensive vehicles.... However vigorously the Anglia might be thrown into a bend it rolls very little, and only violent tactics will induce the tyres to squeal.'

There was some criticism, however, of the front seats: 'A little curvature of the front seat backrests for lateral support would be appreciated; the cushions are rather steeply angled, and their spring rate at times conflicts

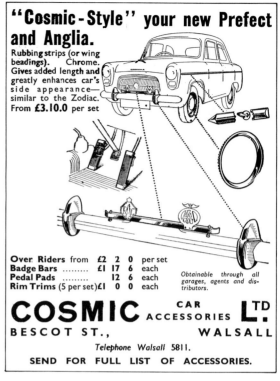
with the excellently phased road springs.' The wiper system, too, came in for criticism: 'An infuriating traditional Ford fitment is the vacuum-type screen-wiper mechanism. Despite a large vacuum reservoir, and however the control valve is set, the blades progressively slow to a complete standstill on full throttle, yet with the same setting on closed throttle they slap violently from side to side at high speed. However, they are certainly powerful.' Nevertheless, *The Autocar* staff were still impressed with the Anglia overall, summing up thus: 'Now very firmly established in the public's favour, the Ford Anglia is the more attractive for its extra luxury of trim and equipment in this De Luxe form. It is a thoroughly honest, robust and roadworthy product with attractive road manners and an agile performance. For those who prefer, or for any reason need, the two-pedal control, this installation is inexpensive and serves its purpose within the limitations already outlined.'

Apart from its obvious benefit to people with certain disabilities, the two-pedal system offered no real advantage for even the uninterested average driver: like similar installations on other cars, it found few buyers when fitted to the small Fords and was therefore deleted as an option a year later. A far better transmission option then, although not available from Ford, was another overdrive unit with mechanical engagement. This was manufactured by the Murray Car Company, of Liverpool. A short, additional gearlever sprouting from the transmission tunnel provided very quick and positive engagement of the overdrive unit in any gear, and when used with second gear it allowed useful overtaking in that ratio up to around 50mph. On top, the overdrive gave 18mph/1,000rpm, allowing the 100E to cruise effortlessly in the 65mph region whilst returning better than 30mpg. All this for a price of £29 included crating and carriage charges, and the unit could be fitted by Ford agents for £5.

The last of the 100E line was the Popular, exemplified by this De Luxe model, still going strong when photographed recently.

By this time, the 100E could no longer claim superiority in respect of performance for this class of car, as the BMC Austin A30 and Morris Minor had 'grown up' sometime previously to become the A35 and Minor 1000, with their new 948cc engines putting them into the genuine 70mph class alongside the small Fords. Nevertheless, the range continued successfully in Anglia and Prefect form until September 1959. Then, the Anglia name was transferred to the all-new 105E model which was ready to go into production, whilst the 100E continued in the guise of the new Ford Popular, replacing the ageing 'upright' 103E model of that name. Once again a detrimming exercise had been undertaken, allowing a very basic 100E Popular to be listed at £494, which, although £80 more expensive than the

Plain door trims and seating and a new, cheaper floor-covering material were to be found inside the 100E Popular. Fixed quarter-lights indicate a standard model: at first even the parcel shelf was an extra, though it soon became part of the standard specification.

discontinued Popular, still made it the cheapest car available in Britain as it undercut the new BMC Mini by just £3. However, a De Luxe Popular, at £515, seemed to offer much better value than the very spartan basic model. Externally, the De Luxe featured chrome-plated embellishments generally in line with the previous Anglia De Luxe, whilst inside the equipment included a parcel shelf, ashtrays, an interior light, twin sunvisors and swivelling front quarter-windows.

A corresponding estate car continued, badged as the Escort, although in fact it was now an amalgamation of features from both the previous Escort and Squire and was an interim model that would be discontinued just as soon as a new 105E Anglia estate became available. Another interim car was the 107E Prefect, which was a 100E shell, trimmed to the De Luxe specification, but powered by the new 105E OHV engine and four-speed gearbox. This 'new' Prefect enabled Dagenham to offer a compact four-door car (the new Anglia was designed strictly round a two-door layout), with the advantages in respect of both performance and mechanical refinement which the 105E engine/gearbox offered, until such time as the new medium-range Fords then under development were announced. Although smaller than the sidevalve unit, the 997cc 105E engine developed more power, and as it was pulling the same overall gearing as before in the Prefect, it gave a small but nevertheless useful increase in performance. At a price of £621 the 107E Prefect was considered quite a bargain. Maximum speed was up only very slightly, but around 3 seconds were shaved off the 0-60mph time, and with 60mph available in third gear the open-road overtaking abilities were much improved. Improvements in the fuel consumption figures, however, were offset somewhat by the new engine's need for Premium-grade fuel, although overall the new Prefect would still be the more economical.

In the event, the 107E had a short production life, being deleted early in 1961 to make way for the Consul Classic 315 which was to bridge the gap between the Anglia and the much larger MK 2 Consul. By this time, also, the 100E Escort had been replaced, leaving just the Popular saloon to continue in both basic and De luxe forms until June 1962, when the last of the sidevalve Fords, a Popular De Luxe, left Dagenham. An extremely inexpensive basic-specification car of obsolete design was not nearly so desirable by this time amongst new-car buyers, and with increasing affluence to be seen all around, the Ford Popular theme had at last outlived its usefulness. It would not be until long after the new generation of Anglias had also gone that an economic downturn would see a Ford Popular listed again.

CHAPTER 4

Sporting
sidevalves

On road, rally and race track

The good performance displayed by the small Fords was due largely to the provision of ample cylinder capacities — particularly in the case of the 10hp — in cars of modest weight. In contrast to the alternative small-car strategy of using small but highly tuned and therefore also highly stressed units, this meant that the Ford sidevalve engines as they left the factory were in a relatively 'lazy' and undeveloped state of tune: in fact, they were rugged enough to withstand considerably greater power outputs than they gave in standard production form, and specialist tuning firms soon began to devise various methods of enhancing Anglia and Prefect performance.

Unfortunately, in the early postwar years, there was little scope for the sporting driver, or anyone else for that matter, to enjoy much performance motoring as the petrol rationing in force did not allow for pleasure use, and virtually eliminated that pastime for quite a while. Nevertheless, 'souped up' cars did begin to appear, and in their issue of January 29, 1947 *The Motor* reported on a hot Prefect which they had recently sampled. In earlier days the small Ford engine had responded well to supercharging, and this Prefect featured a Marshall supercharger which boosted the ingoing mixture with a pressure of 5psi. With the normal gearing retained, the maximum speed, at 65.2mph, was not much improved, but acceleration showed a substantial improvement, 50mph being attained from rest in 18.7 seconds as against 26.9 seconds with a standard car. Overtaking in the supercharged Prefect was much swifter, the 30-50mph time in top gear improving from 18.1 seconds to an excellent 11.5 seconds. Fuel consumption, however, suffered and a 50mph cruising speed returned only 28mpg, some 5 or 6mpg worse than standard. An installation such as this cost £55, with a £2 10s fitting charge, putting up the price of a Prefect so equipped to £409 10s, still usefully cheaper than any other 'ten' on the market.

As postwar shortages eased, motor sport began to flourish once again, and by 1949 the small Fords could be seen contesting events such as the Dutch International Tulip Rally, which was staged for the first time that year. The 1,750-mile road section of the Tulip was not considered to be too severe, and to sort out the finishers eliminating tests were to be held at Zandvoort at the end of the rally, including an acceleration run and a turn around a pylon in the centre of a 29ft circle. Two export Anglias (10hp) and a Prefect were amongst the entries and, anticipating a good run to the

Joy Cooke on her way to collecting the Ladies' Prize in the 1949 Lisbon Rally. Earlier in the year, with Ken Wharton driving and Joy Cooke navigating, ONO 563 had won the Dutch International Tulip Rally outright.

finish, and therefore being in the eliminating tests, their drivers decided to practice handbrake turns before the start of the rally. Unfortunately, this session resulted in two of the Fords being overturned, but some overtime work by mechanics at the Ford agency in The Hague saw them fit to take their place at the start. The practice in fact proved very valuable, as Ken Wharton and co-driver Joy Cooke brought their Anglia in to Zandvoort without penalty. In the final test, Wharton 'handbraked' the Anglia round the pylon in fine style, lifting both inside wheels well clear of the ground before accelerating out of the circle and down the track to the finish and outright victory in the rally. That year, driving the same Anglia, Joy Cooke also won the Ladies Cup in the Lisbon Rally.

Although some sponsorship was provided by Ford, these were not works cars as such, usually being entered by Ford dealerships, such as J. Blake & Company, of Liverpool, whose directors, cousins Jack and Peter Reece, campaigned regularly in Anglias in the early 1950s. In the 1950 Tulip Rally the Reece cousins won the up-to-1,500cc class after Jack Reece took the Anglia through the elimination test at Zandvoort just 0.68 of a second quicker than the Dutch-driven Morgan 4/4 (also 1,172cc Ford-engined) which finished runner-up in the same category. Anglias contesting the Monte Carlo Rally usually finished the course, and were sometimes quite well placed. In the 1952 event, in which more than a third of the entry failed to finish because of the atrocious conditions, a 933cc model driven by D. Murray came third in the up-to 1,100cc class. The following year, in which there were just two classifications — up-to-1,500cc and over — Jack and Peter Reece were amongst the unpenalized cars on arrival at Monte Carlo in their 933cc Anglia, and went on to finish third in the class after the braking and acceleration tests. Commenting recently on the unpenalized road-run, Jack Reece remembered: 'The only reason was because we followed a local driver from Valence to Le Puy in thick fog and managed the stage "clean" — it was only when we arrived at Le Puy we discovered he was drunk!'

By this time, Ford had established a competition department. With the arrival of the 100E range the earlier models quickly disappeared from the international rallying scene, although Ralph Sleigh took a 103E Popular on the 1954 Monte and finished the course, and competition activities at a lower level continued to attract the 'upright' Fords in great numbers. A wide variety of engine tuning equipment was now available for these cars, due in part to the fact that the Ford Ten chassis was the basis for a large number of

Cousins Peter (left) and Jack Reece with their class-winning Anglia on the 1950 Tulip Rally. PTW 832 contested several major events in the early 1950s.

A pair of spotlights, a radiator muff and a roof-rack carrying a spare wheel shod with a snow tyre: necessary wear for the well-equipped rally car — 35 years ago, of course.

An E93A Prefect is put through its paces during the London Motor Club's Little Rally in April 1954.

specials, and tuned Anglias and Prefects — and of course the new 103E Popular — were to be seen frequently in club events.

First-stage engine tuning usually consisted of a twin-carburettor set-up, an inexpensive example of this being offered by the Aquaplane Performance Equipment Company, who could supply a new manifold and an additional Zenith carburettor for £11 15s, the original Zenith carburettor completing the dual arrangement. Twin SU carburettors gave better results, however, and an arrangement in which two semi-downdraught SUs were mounted on short induction pipes attached directly to the inlet ports was offered by the Ace Service Station, on the North Circular Road in North London, and priced at £21.

A 933cc Anglia so equipped was tested by *The Autocar* (November 6, 1953) in whose hands it accelerated from rest to 50mph in 28.7 seconds, a 9.4 seconds improvement over the standard model. Overtaking ability was much improved, the top gear 30-50mph time being reduced by 15 seconds to a respectable 20.7 seconds, and *The Autocar* commented: 'In the 30-to-50mph range, which covers the speeds most frequently in use, the car felt

considerably more lively that a standard model, and there was a notable difference in the way in which the converted car would pull at a good speed up quite stiff inclines in top gear. Engine noise was greater than from a standard model, the engine having a very sharp note when accelerating on full throttle. The difference was not so noticable when cruising, however, even at about a true 50mph. Petrol consumption was satisfactory, being 37mpg when driving at a brisk pace, and falling to 29mpg under severe conditions, constantly using full throttle and driving completely without regard to fuel consumption.'

Other twin SU conversions were available, the one from Aquaplane featuring two 1¼-inch SUs attached to their specially designed inlet manifold being particularly good value at £15 19s. A cast four-branch exhaust manifold for use with this conversion was £5 5s extra. V.W. Derrington Ltd offered a one-piece dual-inlet and four-outlet exhaust manifold complete with twin SUs at £26, their advertisement claiming that this installation would provide 'up to 50% better acceleration and hill-climbing with possible slight extra fuel consumption'.

Two views of an Aquaplane twin-Zenith and four-branch-exhaust conversion, recently rescued from a scrap 1,172cc Ford.

The performance offered by these conversions made them an attractive propostion, but if full use was to be made of the higher octane premium petrols which were becoming available an increase in compression ratio was desirable, and there was considerable scope for achieving this too. Thinner cylinder-head gaskets than the standard Ford copper/asbestos item were available from several specialists, providing a small but useful increase in the compression ratio, the most effective of these being the LMB single-piece steel gasket, which gave a 6.7:1 ratio on the 10hp engines. By fitting an 8hp cylinder-head to a 10hp block the compression ratio was raised to 7.6:1 with a standard Ford gasket, or an ultimate 9:1 with the LMB steel option. Replacement high-compression light-alloy cylinder heads were another alternative, the Derrington Silver Top head for the 8hp and 10hp engines being particularly good value at £8 10s, whilst the Aquaplane alloy Superhead at £11 17 6d was offered in a variety of compression ratios to suit particular needs.

Attempts to increase the power output of a sidevalve engine of given capacity are ultimately limited by the restricted breathing inherent in the layout. One conversion for the Ford Ten which sought to overcome this handicap was the LRG light-alloy cylinder head incorporating overhead inlet valves which appeared in 1955. It was developed initially as a one-off job for the 1,172cc Formula racing car of Frank Nichols, the proprietor of London Road Garage (hence LRG): in racing form, with a 9.5:1 compression ratio and fed by four Amal carburettors, it produced about 65bhp. For road use, however, alternative lower compression ratios were available, along with an inlet manifold designed to take both the original and an additional Zenith carburettor. The standard exhaust manifold could also be retained, and in this guise the conversion provided some 50% more power than the unmodified 10hp engine, although at £65 for the new head alone this was not a cheap option.

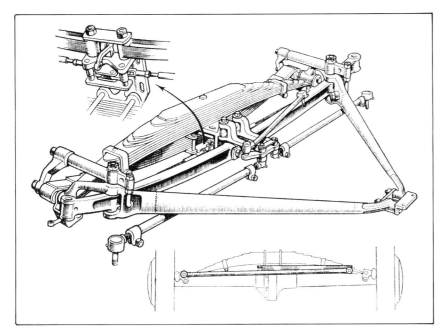

Whilst extracting this sort of output did not seem to harm the engine, problems could certainly arise when using the increased speeds available on the road. The Anglia/Prefect suspension system had never been intended to cope with such a greatly enhanced performance level, and, at the very least, transverse anti-sway bars, such as those manufactured by Stabilizer Products Ltd at £2 18s 6d each, were desirable at both ends of the car, whilst a better although much more expensive solution was to fit independent front suspension.

L.M. (Les) Ballamy had designed a divided beam-axle independent front suspension unit for the small Ford chassis in the 1930s, and more recently a similar system had been offered by the North Downs Engineering Company (also known for their Nordec supercharger

Not the most likely of racing cars! A Model C, its original wire wheels replaced by steel ones, relay racing at Silverstone in company with a Triumph TR.

An LMB-equipped Popular reveals its swing-axle IFS geometry during a six-hour relay race at Silverstone. The angle of roll and the flailing wiper blade indicate a velocity well in excess of what its sedate, upright styling might suggest was normal.

installations). In February 1956, Ballamy announced a new independent front suspension and improved rear suspension conversion at an inclusive exchange price of £37 10s. The conversion utilized several standard Ford components, including the original beam-axle, which was divided centrally and hinged to a bracket located beneath the main spring. The spring itself was 3 inches longer than standard, and ahead of this was an underslung auxiliary helper spring. The front track was also increased by 3 inches, at which the wheels were still nicely inside the arches. At the rear, there was now a 2in longer spring, although the track remained unaltered, and lateral location was provided by a Panhard rod. Just how much these modifications transformed the handling qualities can be judged by comments which appeared in *The Autocar* of March 26, 1956. After having tested an LMB Popular, the magazine noted: 'More sporting folk will rejoice that it now corners in truly classic style with scarcely a trace of roll, and inspires such confidence that one can play enjoyable games of cat-and-mouse on twisty roads with much faster cars.... The engine of the Ford Popular can be tuned to quite a high pitch, and the combination of extra power with these enhanced handling properties would make this an interesting proposition for the sporting motorist who also needs room for the family, yet cannot turn a blind eye to his bank balance.' Les Ballamy campaigned one of these cars himself during the racing season, and a

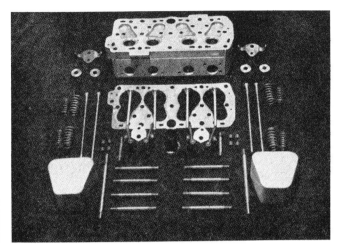
report in *The Autocar* (August 24, 1956) of the 750 Motor Club's six-hour relay handicap race at Silverstone serves to illustrate the ultimate potential of an LMB-sprung Ford, the reporter commenting: 'Leslie Ballamy's Popular, with his own divided front axle suspension and 100E Anglia engine fitted with two Amal carburettors and bunch-of-bananas exhaust manifold, was an eye-opener for many, whistling into Woodcote at nearly 70mph and taking it like a Grand Prix car.'

With the range of equipment available, many enthusiasts were able to tailor a small Ford to suit both their performance requirements and their pocket. A brand new Popular was still only £413, so anyone with £500 to spend could equip one of these with LMB suspension and, for example, an Aquaplane Superhead, twin SUs and a four-branch exhaust, and still have enough change for the £10 road tax, whilst the less well-off enthusiast could always pick up a sound used example, modify it substantially, and be quite competitive at club events. Indeed, the very existence of these cheap, but so very sturdy cars was alone responsible for many people being able to enjoy active participation in motor sport well beyond the 1950s.

As it was even more robust than the original 10hp unit, the 100E engine naturally lent itself well to power tuning, and, because the new Anglias and Prefects possessed roadholding and handling qualities which in the opinion of many experts at that time put them into the sportscar category, a tuned 100E model was a most attractive proposition. Naturally enough, the treatment applied to the 100E engine in the quest for more speed followed the pattern established on the earlier engines, although the differences and lack of interchangeability between the two units necessitated the engineering of new conversions for the 100E.

As had been the case with the earlier 1.172cc engines, an OHIV conversion proved very successful on the 100E unit. LRG had by now adopted the Elva name.

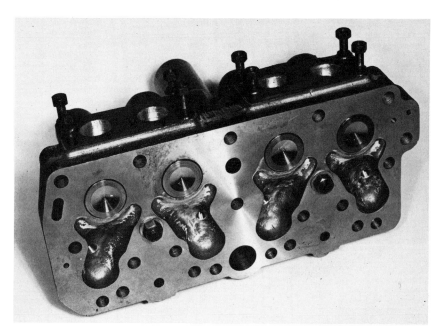

An alternative to the Elva head was this OHIV conversion offered by John Willment. In both cases, two separate rocker covers leave space for the distributor and water take-off between them.

V.W. Derrington offered a modified cylinder head with raised compression ratio and polished combustion chambers, priced at £6 2s 6d, or only £4 if the original head was exchanged. A set of eight inner valve springs to provide a double-valve-spring arrangement were just 7 shillings extra! This equipment alone enabled a 100E model to accelerate from rest to 50mph in 16.8 seconds and to exceed 70mph comfortably. Adding Derrington's combined twin SU/four-branch exhaust manifold conversion, priced at £26, which included the carburettors,would bring a further 2 seconds reduction in the 0-50mph time while allowing an 80mph maximum speed.

Although better-known for their steel-tube spaceframe chassis which took Ford components, Buckler Cars offered a range of tuning equipment equally applicable to specials or saloons.

Another famous name in the tuning business was V. W. Derrington, and useful performance increases could be obtained from a 100E fitted with one of their conversions.

Aquaplane, too, developed various stages of tune, their cheapest conversion, at £12 19s, being a twin-Solex arrangement in which the original Solex was retained along with a second, similar unit. A twin-SU set-up was £17 19s, and a four-branch exhaust manifold offered further improvement for a modest £5 10s. A light-alloy Superhead (£12 15s), racing valve springs (£2), and a high-lift camshaft (£17 19s) were also available. Aquaplane agents Richards & Carr, of London SW1, loaned their demonstration Anglia, equipped with all the options except the high-lift camshaft, which in any case was a racing rather than a road-going modification, to *Autosport*'s John Bolster. In his report, after first

59

A 100E Anglia in action on the London Motor Club's Little Rally in April 1955. An interesting selection of contemporary machinery is visible in the background.

describing the equipment fitted, Bolster continued: 'It will be noticed that the standard camshaft had been retained.... Once one starts going in for fancy timing on a sidevalve engine, the petrol economy is bound to suffer.... On the road, the fuel economy was found to be at least as good as that of a standard Anglia.... My test mileage included crossing London twice, and I recorded 28.3mpg. Any Anglia owner who drives reasonably fast will agree that fitting the speed equipment had not increased the vehicle's thirst. However, this was a performance kit, and certainly the motor had a lot of extra "steam". The mean timed maximum speed was 78.5mph, compared with 72mph for the standard car.... I had a run down-wind at 83.3mph, proving that a genuine "eighty" is always available under only slightly favourable conditions. The engine did not seem to be over-stressed at these high speeds. As regards acceleration, the standing quarter-mile came down to 21.7 seconds... and up to 50mph no less than 4.4 seconds were knocked off, partly because a full 50mph was available on second gear. The 0-60mph time was 22.8 seconds. Thus, the Aquaplane-equipped car was obviously much livelier than any ordinary Anglia. When pressed, the engine was a little more noticeable, but not to an objectionable degree.... The increased acceleration made driving less tiring in heavy traffic, and was a valuable safety feature when overtaking lorries. Nevertheless, the

60

Border checkpoint: Maurice Gatsonides and T. St John Foster with a 100E Anglia on the 1954 Tulip Rally.

increase in performance is not sufficient to render improvements in roadholding necessary.'

Overall, this was an impressive report. But more than this was available as, following the success of the OHIV cylinder head conversion for the earlier 10hp engine, Frank Nichols, in conjunction with gasflow expert Harry Weslake, had developed a similar conversion for the 100E unit. This was eventually marketed in 1956 as the Elva head, Frank Nichols also being the proprietor of the Elva Engineering Company. As before, the cylinder head, which was of 8.9:1 compression ratio, could be used with the existing manifolding and carburettor to give a marked performance increase, for a price of £58 10s. Additionally, of course, twin Solex or SU carburettors could be fitted, as could a four-branch exhaust and a high-lift camshaft.

John Bolster tested an Anglia equipped with the Elva head and twin Solex carburettors. Reporting his findings in *Autosport*, he began by pointing out some of the drawbacks when modifying a sidevalve engine, noting that: 'Provided that a "moderate" camshaft and a not too efficient manifold are employed, the fuel consumption of the sidevalve unit is acceptable. Any attempt to use ramming pipes or an extractor exhaust system, however, may result in an absurd thirst for petrol and little else. The reason, of course, is that part of the charge goes straight from the inlet valve to the exhaust during overlap, without pausing to visit the cylinder. Those amateurs who have tuned their Anglias not wisely but too well now know why they only get 17mpg !'

After describing the Elva head, he turned to the car in question, which 'had covered 42,000 miles, of which 18,000 were after conversion and

'Gatso' hustles the Anglia on round the Nürburgring towards victory in the 1.300cc GT class, 1954 Tulip Rally.

included some successful racing. Apart from the head, stronger clutch springs had been fitted, and a pair of Buckler constant-mesh gears stepped up the indirect ratios.... The acceleration and maximum speed are considerably better than those of last year's Zephyr (Mk1), in fact they approach those of the current "Six" (Mk2). However, to get the performance figures in their true perspective, it is best to compare them with a standard car of the same model.... I have all the stopwatch figures for a well-prepared specimen. These appear in brackets after those of the Elva-modified car. The maximum speed was 83.3mph (72mph), and the time for the standing quarter-mile 20.2secs (23.2). The acceleration figures, on a recalibrated speedometer, were 0-30mph 4.6secs (5.8), 0-50mph 10.8secs (15.4) and 0-60mph 16.6secs (26.0). The 0-70mph figure was 27.2secs, and was not, of course, taken on the original car. Thus, the improvement in performance is so great that it is of a different order altogether.'

Although air cleaner/silencers were fitted to the carburettors, John Bolster thought: 'the engine could still be heard and felt more than a standard unit', although 'the slightly "harder" character of the Elva-modified version does not reach objectionable levels.' Overall, it appears that the economy level would be about the same as the standard car, with an improvement of around 3mpg being evident if the Elva car were cruised at normal 100E speeds. In respect of handling qualities, the Elva-modified engine did apparently stretch the Anglia to its limits, Bolster commenting that 'With all this extra power, though, the roadholding begins to get a bit ragged at the edges, and one is conscious of a bouncing back axle on occasions. As tested by me, the car was perfectly controllable if a little skittish, but I would prefer to tighten up the suspension a bit before fitting those big SUs, and that camshaft.' Finally, it was evident that Bolster had thoroughly enjoyed himself whilst testing the Elva Anglia, as he concluded: 'Nothing could appear less like a sportscar than this little square box. For this reason, the look of incredulity on the faces of other drivers is alone worth the price of the Elva conversion.'

A particularly potent Anglia about this time, which it seems likely was destined to remain a one-off job, was one converted by well-known racing car builder Cyril Kieft. At the request of one of Kieft's customers, a Coventry Climax 1,100cc engine in unit with an MG TC gearbox was installed in the Anglia. With approximately 75bhp available, this Anglia would probably have been a genuine 90mph car. Modifications to the radiator were necessary to accommodate the slightly longer Coventry Climax engine, and although Kieft apparently did not convert any more cars he did offer the conversion in kit form, including adaptor plates, fittings etc, at £298. Whether any kits were sold, however, is not clear.

The 100E Anglia made its international rallying debut in the RAC Rally in March 1954, with the cars of Robin Richards and Norman Quick taking

With hooded headlamps too,
and a deflector across the back
of the bonnet to direct warm air
from the engine compartment
over the screen – an effective
de-icer – Edward Harrison's
Anglia negotiates the Col de
Turini on its way to Monte Carlo
in 1956.

Harrison on the 1956 Monte
again, swinging the Anglia into a
hairpin in the mountains.

first and second places in the up-to-1,300cc Touring Car class. The Manufacturer's Team Prize, too, went to Ford, the reserve works team in which the Anglias of Nancy Mitchell and Jack Reece were teamed up with T.C. 'Cuth' Harrison's Zephyr being the winners.

After this, preparations were quickly put in hand for the Dutch International Tulip Rally in which two nominated Ford teams, each consisting of an Anglia, a Consul and a Zephyr, were competing, one of the teams being equipped with modified cars, whilst the others remained standard. Dutchman Maurice Gatsonides, who had won the Monte Carlo Rally for Ford with a Zephyr the previous year, was to drive the modified Anglia. At this stage, in March/April 1954, the tuning specialists were not yet marketing conversions for the 100E, so the engine of 'Gatso's' Anglia, XVX 161, was sent to Ford's new experimental engineering department at Rainham. Here, considerable work was carried out on the cylinder head, valves, inlet/exhaust ports and camshaft, and with twin carburettors and a Lucas racing coil the engine was said to be as 'hot' as Ford could make it. Other modifications included a straight-through silencer, windscreen washers, electric windscreen wipers, a louder horn and an engine temperature gauge. Suspension modifications were confined to binding the rear spring leaves very tightly together with string, as 'Gatso' preferred this method of stiffening up the car, having used it successfully on his Monte Carlo Zephyr, to the more usual expedient of adding an extra leaf. Binding the springs this way causes them to act in a more consistently controlled manner by stopping the leaves from separating, and is therefore of particular benefit during violent cornering tactics especially on indifferent surfaces.

Completing XVX 161's equipment was a reclining passenger seat. A comprehensive tool/spares kit consisting of a coil, choke cable, fuel pump, fan belt, radiator filler cap, top and bottom hoses, six spark plugs, a set of engine gaskets, a socket set, a tin of brake fluid, six wheel nuts, two CO^2 bottles, two wheel braces, a tyre pump, and a Smiths Bevelift jack was

RAC Rally, March 1956: rather more spring-like weather has enabled the winter equipment to be removed from 966 EPU. Edward Harrison negotiates a special test on Blackpool Promenade.

65

Jeff Uren takes his new Anglia on an early outing at Brands Hatch. His own comment – 'Note: not yet serious, bumpers, badges and all. No crash hat yet.'

Getting more serious: Jeff has applied 'stage one' tuning to the Anglia – removing the bumpers, badge-bar and grille! The date is June 1956, the track is Silverstone, and the Anglia is overtaking the Morgan.

added to the standard Anglia toolkit. All this preparation certainly paid off, as Gatsonides and co-driver T. St John Foster drove the Anglia to victory in the up-to-1,300cc GT class, completing a hat-trick for Ford in the event as Jack Reece (Consul) and Denis Scott (Zephyr) each won their respective classes. The standard model Anglia entered, however, had not fared so well, finishing seventh in the up-to-1,300cc Touring Car class, which was dominated by the rather more powerful and appreciably lighter Fiat 1100TV models.

Later in the year, the Anglias gave a particularly good account of themselves in the 1,230 mile MCC/Redex National Rally, which included several trials-type sections turned into quagmires in the November rains. The Team Prize in the Production Touring Car category went to the nominated Anglia team of D. Edwards, E. Baker, and P.J. Anton, whilst the Anglias of B. Warr, P.J. Anton, and Dr C. Hardman took first, second and third places, respectively, in the up-to-1,300cc Closed Car class. Mrs Yvonne Jackson took the Ladies Prize in her Anglia, and the modified Anglia of A.M. Reed combined with the Consul of L. Gibbs and H. Thomas' Zephyr to win the Supercharged and Special Cars team award.

At this time, the Anglias were the second-string cars in so far as the Ford competition department were concerned, and so therefore did not always contest the major international events as works cars. Nevertheless, the privately entered Anglias of E.V. Baker and R.N. Richards took first and third places, respectively, (a Fiat 1100 was second) in the 1,300cc Production Touring Car category on the 1955 RAC Rally, an excellent result in an event described in *The Motor*'s report as 'The toughest rally ever run in this country'. The snow which had gripped Britain at the time of the RAC Rally in March had given way to better conditions in April when the Midland Automobile Club staged its annual Birmingham Post Rally, a national event over a 400-mile route, which attracted 160 entrants. The Production Touring Cars were split into three classes, with Class B embracing cars from 1,001 to 2,000cc, not exactly an ideal classification for the 1,172cc-engined Fords. Nevertheless, P.J. Anton won this class in his Anglia, a creditable performance also coming from the second-placed Volkswagen (1,192cc), with a more likely-looking MG Magnette being kept back in third place. Ford works driver Denis Scott had entered his own

Jeff Uren in action in 1957 with the ex-Ian Walker Prefect. An additional anti-roll bar can be seen clamped below the standard fitting to stiffen the front suspension.

Anglia in this event, but after setting up the fastest class time in the first special test, he failed to repeat the performance in the remainder, and went out of the reckoning.

Two weeks later, Scott was back in action at international level, taking a modified, works-entered Anglia on the Tulip Rally. The first of the special stages was a 35-mile narrow twisting climb and descent in the Black Forest. One of *The Autocar*'s reporters positioned himself near a hairpin bend on the climb: if he was anticipating some drama, he cannot have been disappointed as he reported: 'A tremendous blasting of horns announced the arrival of two Chevrolets and a Ford Customline, who were being held up by a non-competing Volkswagen. It started to rain and, higher up, Blockley's Austin Healey lay sadly by the side of the road, an early casualty with a gearbox that "went bang". At the hairpin there came another bang as the TD MG driven by A. Bouwmeester slid and nosed into the bank. Just to show how it should be done, the Ford Anglia of Scott and Hardman went round like a flash, valves bouncing, tail sliding, to vanish up the hill in a cloud of spray.' Denis Scott continued well, actually putting up third fastest time of any competitor in one of the later special stages which consisted of a timed descent of a twisting mountain pass. Nevertheless, narrowly leading the class at the end, with just the final test to undergo — 10 laps of the Zandvoort Grand Prix circuit — was Keisel's modified Renault, and the little French car kept its lead despite Scott's indulging in some three-wheel cornering at Zandvoort. Third in the class was another Anglia, privately entered by a French crew. In September, locally entered Fords dominated the Pretoria-Lourence Rally in South Africa, a three-day long reliability trial over unmade third-class roads. Of the 101 starters, only 57 survived the course, an Anglia taking outright victory and combining with a Prefect and a Zephyr to win the Manufacturer's Team Prize.

Three works Anglias contested the 1956 Monte Carlo Rally, all running in the standard category. After co-driving for his father, Cuth Harrison, for the previous two years, Edward Harrison was having his first 'fully fledged' works drive in one of the Anglias, and succeeded in bringing it in to the finish in 15th place overall, the highest placed of any of the Fords at Monte Carlo that year, and three places ahead of his father's Zodiac! In April, a locally entered Anglia won the small-car class in the East African Safari, and in July, an Anglia scored another outright win in Africa. This was in the Ndola Rally, staged over a 1,800-mile route of unpaved tracks in Southern Rhodesia, the severity of which eliminated 13 of the 38 starters. Both the Manufacturer's Team Prize and an Open Team Prize went to Ford, as the only intact team entry amongst the finishers was a nominated team of two Anglias and a Zephyr.

More than anything else, perhaps, it is these African results which confirm the 100E's rugged qualities, as these locally entered cars were

A Willment OHIV cylinder head and a large Solex carburettor provided super-power for the Ian Walker/Jeff Uren 100E Prefect, 760 CMU.

A 100E Anglia, with a clearly-visible add-on anti-roll bar helping to keep it well under control, during the 1957 six-hour relay race at Silverstone: above, leading a Goggomobil coupe (unlikely cars were a delightful feature of these races) and right, kicking up a rear wheel while keeping a Morris 1000 at bay.

almost always competing against strong Volkswagen entries in the small-car classes, the sturdy construction of the German Beetle making it, too, a popular car in Africa. This situation was very evident in the 1958 East African Safari, when, at the end of the gruelling 2,900-mile route, the Anglia of T. Brooke and Peter Hughes had won the small-car class just ahead of four Volkswagens, with another Anglia in sixth place.

Back home, the 100E range was extremely popular amongst enthusiasts as an inexpensive competition car ideal for club races and rallies. A popular event at Silverstone each year was the 750 Motor Club's six-hour relay race in which several four-car teams competed. Handicapping was worked out on the basis of awarding credit laps to each team according to the cars' performance potential, with a minimum number of laps specified for each car in the team. Usually, teams consisted of one make, or even one model, but in the 1955 event a 'Tinlids' team consisting of a Fiat 1100TV, a Volkswagen and two 100Es contested the event. Being composed of relatively low-powered cars (Austin-Healeys and TR2s were amongst the

37 teams entered), the Tinlids started with 41 credit laps. With the most credit laps, and therefore starting in the lead, were the Morris Minor team, but after $3\frac{1}{2}$ hours of racing the Tinlids emerged out in front and were still there half-an-hour from the end when the MG TD/TF team came through into second place. Although the MGs continued to close the gap, the Tinlids held on, and at the end it was Ian Walker's Prefect, devoid of hubcaps in true racing style, but nevertheless on whitewall tyres, that took the chequered flag.

After co-driving for his brother in the 1955 Monte Carlo Rally, in which they competed in an Armstrong-Siddeley, Jeff Uren, who was later to win the Saloon Car Championship for Ford with the MK2 Zephyr and become better-known in the 1960s for his remarkable 3-litre V6 Cortina Savages, ordered a new 100E Anglia with which to start his own competition driving

career. Anglias, however, were in somewhat short supply in 1955, with 8 months delivery being quoted, but the resourceful Jeff Uren somehow managed to procure an Anglia with which he gained a class win in the London Motor Club's Little Rally. Later in the year the new Anglia, XPD 694, arrived and contested the Plymouth Presidential Rally before having a taste of the big-time as a private entry in the 1956 Monte. Some circuit racing followed, and Jeff's 100E joined forces with three others (one of which was a van!) to form the Scuderia Throttolo Bendori team which contested the 1956 Silverstone six-hour relay. In the race, the 'Throttle Benders' didn't manage to repeat the performance of the previous year's Tinlids, a team of MG Magnettes taking the honours this time with the Fords in a creditable fourth place just ahead of the AC Owners' Club team.

Whilst these antics were taking place at Silverstone, the Ulster Automobile Club were staging their annual hill-climb at Craigantlet. The

Anne Hall hurries her works Anglia through one of the special stages on the RAC Rally in 1958. The similar Fords of F. Grounds and A. Hartnell finished second and third in the 1,001-to-1,300cc Normal Series Production Touring Saloon category.

71

100Es of R. Draper and Paddy Hopkirk recorded 103.68 and 103.70 seconds, times which whilst not quite sufficient to beat N. O'Flaherty's Volkswagen, were good enough to give them second and third place in the 851 to 1,500cc Production Saloon class, which included a Sunbeam Rapier and a Jowett Javelin amongst other contestants.

1957 saw Jeff Uren regularly in action at the wheel of a much modified Prefect, 760 CMU, which had previously been campaigned successfully by Ian Walker, whilst another notable 100E that year was A.J.C. Mackay's supercharged Anglia. Mackay was in the Production Touring Car race at the Brands Hatch Boxing Day meeting which rounded-off the season. From the grid, Tommy Sopwith's Equipe Endeavour 3.4 Jaguar went straight into the lead and was never troubled. Behind the leading Jaguar however, was, as *The Autocar* reported, an epic 'three-cornered battle between Sir G. Baillie in the Equipe's other Jaguar 3.4, Mackay's blown Anglia and Scott Brown suffering rare indignity in an Alfa Romeo 1900 — in that order. The Ford's uncommon urge was matched by its cornering powers and driver's ability; time and again he tried to overtake the Jaguar on the inside at Kidney Bend whilst Scott Brown attacked from the outside.Each time the Jaguar escaped as the bend's radius eased, but after ten laps it had not gained an inch.'

It speaks volumes for the 100E as a racing saloon to be able to record that, although he contested the first BRSCC Saloon Car Championship in 1958 with his Mk2 Zephyr, Jeff Uren continued to race his Prefect regularly in other events. Summing up the 100E recently, Jeff remembered: 'You could abuse it and do terrible things, but never did anything break... literally, you could throw it into a corner, yet I never spun in a 100E.'

Unlike its successor, the 105E model, the 100E has not appeared in large numbers in the Classic Saloon events of more recent years although Keith Rainish competed in a Willment-modified car early on, and subsequently Kevin Owen has raced a 100E Anglia. An Elva 0HIV cylinder head, larger valves and a full race camshaft form the basis for the increased power output of this car, with, at first, a single SU carburettor, then a twin-choke Dellorto, and finally two of these. A balanced crankshaft and a strapped centre main bearing cap allow 7,000rpm to be used: in conjunction with the 4.7:1 rear axle and 6.20 x 13 Avon tyres, that corresponds to 102mph in top and has in fact been seen along Silverstone's club straight. A Ford 2000E gearbox is used with a light-alloy bellhousing. Ford Classic front struts and disc brakes are featured at the front, whilst at the rear are decambered leaf springs and Spax adjustable shock absorbers. At the time of writing, this car is awaiting some rebuilding before further action is contemplated.

CHAPTER 5

The Anglia 105E

Overhead valves and four speeds

Serious thinking at Dagenham about the replacement for the 100E range first took place in 1956, at which time a good, hard look was taken at rival products in the small-car sector. At this time the now famous Ford product planning department was in its infancy, and the new Anglia would be the first of a whole new range of models conceived by this department. An early decision that the rather noticeable gap which existed within the Ford range between the Prefect and the Mk2 Consul should be filled with a new, medium-sized car, enabled those responsible for the 100E replacement to scheme out a compact vehicle designed exclusively around a two-door layout.

Executive engineer Fred Hart was the man with overall responsibility for the new Anglia 105E, and he recalled recently how Company Chairman Sir Patrick Hennessy considered that all too often the rear seat passengers in small cars were rather less well catered for than those in the front, and so, bearing this in mind, close attention was to be paid to the rear seat accommodation in the new model. To this end, a wider door opening than on the two-door 100E was provided, giving easier access to the rear, and the reverse-slope rear window was introduced, this particular feature allowing a longer roof and much improved headroom in the back. Paradoxically, the arrangement actually allowed a slightly lower roof line than previously, so helping the car's aerodynamics slightly. In fact, the drag factor was carefully looked at during the design stage, and the new Anglia's sloping bonnet style was the result of wind-tunnel testing, although, as engineer Hart was well aware, the family car is inevitably something of a compromise, and aerodynamic considerations were not allowed to overrule the more important matters of passenger accommodation and convenience.

Based on a wheelbase $3\frac{1}{2}$in longer than the 100E's, the new shell was, however, slightly narrower than before outside whilst still managing to provide the same internal width. Constructionally, the new bodywork differed considerably from that of the previous Anglia, as experience with both the 100E and the original Consul/Zephyr range had shown that useful weight savings by comparison with these could be attained whilst still retaining the excellent structural strength and rigidity which was a notable feature of Dagenham's first monocoque cars. Very sturdy inner front wings incorporated a turret-like arrangement to house the front suspension upper mountings, from where the suspension loads were transmitted rearwards to a scuttle/bulkhead structure rather less massive-looking than previously, but still very substantial. The steel floor was braced by crossmembers at either end of the passenger area, these transverse members carrying the jacking points at their extremities. Longitudinal box-section members at either side contributed to beam stiffness, and were carried up and over the wheelarch pressings at the rear. An unusually large luggage compartment for a car of this size was provided, both the 7-gallon fuel tank and spare wheel having been repositioned, the former now residing beneath the boot floor whilst the spare wheel was situated in an upright position across the car behind the rear seat bulkhead. A well formed in the boot floor located the wheel, which was secured in position by a strap. Dagenham's usual rather high back panel, styled to house the number-plate, contributed usefully to the car's rear-end rigidity. A self-supporting strut held the large boot lid securely in the open position.

Hinged at its forward edge, the bonnet, too, was self-supporting. The large bonnet top contained the heater air intake grille just ahead of the windscreen. The heater unit, still an optional extra and placed high on the forward sloping scuttle, was the most prominent underbonnet feature. The engine compartment layout was good, care having been taken to ensure that those items needing regular attention were readily accessible. Overall, this new bodyshell represented a considerable achievement, for it offered at least as much accommodation and convenience as the preceding Anglia, and in certain respects more, yet was more compact externally and gave a useful saving in weight. This latter consideration, however, had not been achieved at the expense of structural strength. Indeed, prototype testing carried out in Kenya was so successful as to lead some members of the design team to forecast correctly that the new Anglia would be a formidable contender in the East African Safari Rally.

Basic and De Luxe models were to be offered, the De Luxe car being easily identified externally with its full-width plated grille, bright metal windscreen surround, chrome side strips and plated rear lamp surrounds. The interior appointments were both functional and cheerful. The seating and door trims were in PVC, two-tone on the De Luxe, which also had rayon-weave or leather as a seating option. The front seat squabs were of

The Consul Classic was the new medium-sized car which allowed Ford designers to concentrate exclusively on a two-door layout for the 105E Anglia, the two models having in common a backward-raked rear window. .

74

double curvature, offering useful support to the occupants during cornering. Both front seats were hinged to tip forward and so ease entry to the rear, but only that on the driver's side was given fore-and-aft adjustment. Facing the driver was a deeply-dished two-spoke steering wheel, the spokes being adorned with chrome mouldings on the De Luxe model. A stalk control sprouted from either side of the steering column, the one on the left being the headlamp dipswitch whilst the other operated both the direction indicators and the horn. The neat facia panel featured a large futuristic-looking speedometer ahead of the driver incorporating a fuel gauge and, on the De Luxe car only, an engine temperature gauge. The instrument was set in a larger bright metal panel, the shape of which was repeated for the glove-box situated ahead of the passenger seat and lidded on the De Luxe car. Twin sunvisors and, at last, electric windscreen wipers were standard equipment, as were winding windows and positive-locking opening quarterlights in both doors. Additional on the De Luxe were opening rear side windows, these being hinged at the front and secured at their rear edge by a thief-proof catch. A vinyl roof lining and a moulded rubber floor covering were features of both models.

Predictably enough, the new Anglia's running gear followed what was by that time Dagenham's well-established practice, with MacPherson struts mounted at the top in the front inner wings and located at the bottom by track control arms and a transverse anti-roll bar. Burman steering gear was once again employed, but now with the extremely light-to-operate recirculating-ball steering box. At the rear, the longitudinally mounted half-elliptic leaf springs were considerably longer than on the previous model, being intended to offer both a softer ride and improved roadholding. The axle was offset $1\frac{1}{2}$in forward from the spring centre, and with rubber bump stops set above the spring between the axle line and the front mounting points, spring wind-up was reduced. Armstrong lever-arm shock absorbers completed the rear suspension. Girling hydraulic brakes of the same dimensions as the preceding Anglia were considered quite sufficient for the rather lighter new model, as were the 5.20 x 13 wheel and tyre sizes, although the rims themselves were new, their four fixing studs now being closer to the hub centre.

A simpler frontal treatment, with a narrower grille and less chrome, was adopted for the standard model. 286 DRK is a preserved example photographed recently.

286 DRK shows off the Anglia's distinctive rear-end. Its most striking styling feature, the rearward-sloping back window, helped to provide plenty of headroom for rear-seat passengers.

Under the new Anglia's bonnet was what many small-Ford enthusiasts had been hoping for more than anything else, a completely new overhead-valve, 997cc engine. In October 1956, after a two-year experimental programme, design work had begun on a production 1-litre engine intended to be the smallest capacity unit of a whole range of engines designed around certain common measurements, these being the bore diameter and the bore centres. By standardizing these two dimensions it would be possible to manufacture engines of various capacities from one common cylinder block simply by fitting alternative crankshafts of differing throw. With this in mind, the bore size chosen, 80.96mm, was very large by 1-litre standards, but would have allowed capacities of up to 1,390cc for future models whilst still retaining substantially oversquare dimensions in a block measuring just $7\frac{1}{4}$in in height. In the event, 1,340cc was to be the maximum capacity produced from the original block: the subsequent advent of an additional transfer line at Dagenham allowed a very slightly taller block to be produced around the same bore size and centres, permitting a further increase in stroke, which resulted in the 1.5-litre five-bearing unit. Despite large bores, the new Anglia cylinder block featured water jacketing completely surrounding each cylinder, an arrangement which results in a rather long engine, but virtually guarantees freedom from thermal distortion and head gasket problems which sometimes afflict engines with siamesed bores. A piston stroke of 48.41mm was all that was necessary to achieve the desired 1-litre capacity, the actual figure being 996.6cc, although 997cc is usually quoted.

Interior of an Anglia De Luxe. The chrome cappings on the steering wheel spokes were soon deleted because they caused dazzle and unwelcome reflections in the windscreen. On the standard model, which was without the parcel shelf, the glove box had no lid.

Brian Hatton's cutaway drawing reveals the design features of the 997cc 105E engine, the first of the enormously successful range of 'Kent' power units designed by Ford engineer Alan Worters. The short-stroke dimensions, hollow crankshaft and ample water jacketing are evident. Reproduced by kind permission of Motor.

These dimensions made the engine unusually oversquare by production car standards, with a stroke/bore ratio of 0.6:1. For comparison, two other contemporary small-car engines, the BMC A-series (Austin A35, Morris Minor 1000) and the Standard 10 both shared undersquare bore and stroke measurements of 63mm x 76mm, giving a capacity of 948cc with a stroke/bore ratio of 1.2:1. This characteristic of the 105E engine was later to prove of great interest to tuners, as it made for a high-revving, free-breathing unit. At first, though, it was a matter of production engineering: it enabled an unusually robust crankshaft to be provided, notable for its bearing journal overlap and its hollow construction (a hollow shaft had appeared in the German Ford Taunus engines in 1954 and Dagenham had adopted hollow webs for the Mk2 Consul/Zephyr range of 1956). The considerable overlap of bearing journals, with diameters of 2.125in for the three mains and 1.937in for the big-ends, ensured extreme rigidity and this, coupled with the low inertia loads associated with a short-stroke low-

piston-speed unit, meant that counterweights were unnecessary. The steel-backed bearing shells were lined with white-metal for the mains, with copper-lead being used for the big-ends.

The cast-iron eight-port cylinder head gave a compression ratio of 8.9:1, and featured bathtub combustion chambers which were accurately machined all over, giving very closely controlled volumes. The overhead valves were set vertically and in-line, the exhaust valves being of two-piece construction with the steel-alloy head butt-welded to the stem. Single valve springs were fitted, and the valves were operated in the conventional manner by mushroom tappets, pushrods and rockers, the tappets being offset slightly against the cams to ensure rotation and avoid localized wear. The distributor and oil pump drive gear was cut directly into the camshaft, and drove an external oil pump which was in unit with the oil filter, this arrangement being chosen so as to allow differing shape sump pans if necessary in future model applications of the same basic engine. A camshaft-driven mechanical fuel pump fed a single Solex carburettor mounted on a cast four-branch inlet manifold, and in this configuration the new small-Ford engine produced 39bhp (nett) at 5,000rpm, at which point piston speed was a mere 1,588ft/min, with a peak torque of 52.6lb/ft being developed reasonably well down the revolution range at 2,700rpm. The torque curve, in fact, very closely matched that of the superseded 1,172cc unit between 1,000 and 3,500rpm whilst showing an improvement at higher speeds.

The 7¼in diameter clutch was hydraulically operated, and behind this was the first four-speed gearbox to appear on a Dagenham car. Executive engineer Fred Hart remembers some difficulty in persuading the company to accept a four-speed gearbox as, although there was certainly concern at Dagenham by 1956 over the company's old-fashioned image in respect of its sidevalve-engined small-car range, it was nevertheless thought that at least one traditional Ford feature should be retained if possible. In the event, the arguments for the benefits bestowed upon a small-engined car by a four-speed gearbox won the day, and the opportunity was taken to provide the new Anglia with a set of well-chosen ratios which would allow 35mph and 60mph quite comfortably in second and third gears respectively, with maximums appreciably above these. Synchromesh was provided between the upper three ratios only, so a downward change into first gear whilst on the move would still require some skill in the art of

Anglia at speed: the developing motorway network made the high-revving, smooth-cruising performance of the 105E increasingly welcome.

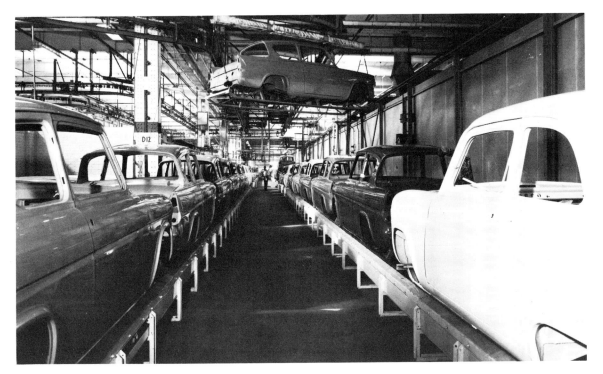

Anglia production at Dagenham. The bodyshells were welded, painted and fully trimmed before being lowered onto the mechanical components on the final assembly lines. A solitary 100E shell indicates Popular production continuing alongside the newer design.

This estate car conversion by Friary Motors of Basingstoke appeared in June 1961. The lift-up tailgate was made from two glassfibre mouldings back-to-back, with moulded-in reinforcement plates for the lock and hinge mountings. Carried out to order on customers' existing cars, the conversion cost £89 12s 6d. Period photo suggests that it had neat proportions, but it remained something of a rarity.

double-declutching. Otherwise, gearchanging would be a pleasure with the short, light-to-operate and very accurate floor-mounted lever. A new hypoid-bevel final drive unit with a ratio of 4.125:1 gave 16.07mph/1,000rpm on top gear, a figure which suggested a maximum in excess of 75mph and certainly higher than usual cruising speeds for this class of car.

Prototype testing was undertaken on an almost global basis, with 30 cars involved in a 500,000-miles test programme in territories where much had been learned in the past with previous Ford models. As has already been mentioned, some prototypes visited East Africa, the unmade roads of Kenya particularly being regarded as ideal for testing not only suspension units, but also the bodyshell's rigidity, whilst the extremely dusty atmosphere in the dry season there was useful for checking out dust-proofing. Northern Scandinavia was used extensively for winterization

Ford launched an estate version of the Anglia in the autumn of 1961. This De luxe model has the optional overriders and whitewall tyres.

82

In 1962, E. D. Abbott, an associate company of Friary Motors, took over the estate car conversion, lowering the price slightly by retaining the saloon's rear side windows. The total cost was still £13 higher than the factory-built equivalent, though.

trials, and the new heater unit designed specifically for the Anglia was one direct result of that experience. High-speed testing was carried out both on German autobahns and American freeways, whilst much endurance testing took place at the company's own facilities in Britain.

Although the announcement date was set for September 1959, production models were leaving the Dagenham assembly lines as early as June that year, a pre-launch build-up having been planned that would enable Ford agents throughout the country not only to show Anglias on release day, but also to sell them right away. In July, sales executives from Ford agencies worldwide were invited to stay in Britain for a week, during which they would have an opportunity to try out production cars in great

The front half of the Anglia estate, back to the centre pillar, was identical to the saloon. The new rear bodywork, with a large lift-up tailgate, blended smoothly with it, avoiding the 'afterthought' look of some other estate cars.

secrecy at the Crystal Palace circuit. So successful was this exercise that an initial order from America for 35,000 new Anglias was placed immediately, and orders already placed by European agencies were more than doubled over the week. This pre-launch production period was also useful in that it allowed random production cars to be tested in routines similarly rigorous to those inflicted on the prototypes before the model was made available to the public.

Unveiling for the benefit of the motoring press took place at London's Grosvenor House on Wednesday, September 9, three weeks before the Anglia's official public launch date. Company Chairman Sir Patrick Hennessy did the honours at the press reception, saying in his speech before revealing the Anglia: 'Now you all know when a company like ours sets out to design a new motor car, we do market research at home and abroad in as many countries as we can, and certainly in all the volume countries, and when we did this research of ours some years ago, we found in fact that what was wanted in one country or another varied very little. Indeed, the specification for Bangkok was pretty close to what they wanted in Birmingham. We found they wanted durability, fuel economy, room and comfort, safety, roadability, performance, and a style which would give them pride of ownership. We've tried to meet that specification and I must tell you that we have not attempted to make a bubble car, nor have we tried to make an austerity car. Nor indeed have we tried to make an ugly car, because as you've seen in recent years we place no premium on ugliness as such.

'You also know — and bear with me when I say these things — that the testing place, the battle ground, as far as the British motor industry is concerned, is in Europe. It is there we have the severest competition. Any car that we make in this country, whoever makes it, that hasn't got a volume potential in Europe, isn't doing a real job for the country. We think the cars we're going to show you have. Now we ought to know something about this, because in 1958 — we haven't got the '59 figures yet, although the first few months are the same — in 1958 we sold 58% of all the small cars exported from this country to Europe. And that's against all the cars which you know are made in this country in the small-car class. Now we're going to double what we've done, in 1960. But don't think we've neglected other markets because at the same time we shipped to the United States of America 66% of all the small cars in the classes which we are talking of. So we know something about the requirements of this class of car in various countries.

'Now in this new Anglia the only thing that is left of the old Anglia is the name. So you and we today are saying goodbye to a very old friend, and it is now my privilege to present to you the world's most exciting light car.'

Three weeks later, on Wednesday, September 30, the 105E Anglia was public knowledge, and in their issue of October 2, *The Autocar* published a full road test report of the De Luxe model which, at £610, was £21 dearer

An export model estate car fitted with window covers enabling it to be used as a van.

Estate-style interior appointments of the export van/estate hybrid. The rear seat cushion tipped forwards and the squab folded flat for maximum luggage space with a flat floor.

An Anglia Super shows off its contrasting colour side stripe. The 1,200cc Anglias bore the designation 123E.

than the basic car, these prices corresponding almost exactly with the two-door Morris Minor at £590 and £619 for the basic and De Luxe, respectively. Commenting on the new engine, *The Autocar* said: 'The very short piston travel per revolution leads one to expect that the engine will rev freely, and so it does; in fact it thrives on high revs.... The exceptionally high third gear maximum of 71mph is equivalent to some 6,300rpm, and at this speed there is still no vibration nor sounds of valve thrash and buzzing — nothing in fact, to prevent an owner from using on occasion the high revs available.... The smoothness at high revs is almost uncanny. In normal driving 30mph in second gear and 60mph in third are readily available, and the speed range in third gear makes this an ideal ratio for overtaking as well as for fairly sustained use in traffic. At all speeds the level of engine noise is commendably low, and a long run is made appreciably less tiring by the quietness of the power unit and the other working components. Any speed up to the near-80mph maximum may be sustained indefinitely, without any impression that it is too fast for the car.' It was noted, however, that: 'The high-speed smoothness of the engine is not repeated, unfortunately, at the bottom end of the rev range. When accelerating below 20mph in top gear the engine is decidedly lumpy... and it is essential that free use be made of the gearbox if the car is to give of its best. Happily, the driver is encouraged to do this by a gearbox which is very pleasant to use. The new four-speed gearbox has well-chosen ratios, each intended to be used to the

Interior details of a 123E Super. Carpeted floor, padded facia top with 'Super' designation, and standard equipment windscreen washer pump are amongst the distinguishing features.

full; thus, bottom gear is rightly needed to start from rest. The synchromesh is powerful, and enables the lever to be whipped across from one gear position to another almost as quickly as the hand can move.' Of the steering gear, it was reported that: '... it is rather too low-geared for full precision of control in the straight ahead position', although: 'There is no tendency to wander on the straight.' Of the ride and handling, the test staff thought that: 'The ride which the car gives is very comfortable, and there is little of the firm vertical movements often associated with small cars.... On corners some roll occurs, but the speed at which they can be taken is remarkably high. The driver always has the car fully under control.... The car understeers noticeably, but in extreme conditions of very hard cornering the back can be made to slip outwards. Adhesion is little reduced when cornering on a wet road, and the Anglia still feels very safe'. Rear seat

comfort, and legroom particularly, came in for praise, but this was tempered with the comment: 'For the driver, less space is available. The pendant pedals locate his feet a few inches from the toeboard, and he does not need to be particularly tall to find his knees arguing with the steering wheel, and interfering with his use of the indicator switch.' This Anglia had accelerated from rest to 50 and 60mph in 17.8 and 29.4 seconds respectively, and covered the 30-50mph and 40-60mph range in third gear in 10.5 and 15.6 seconds, these latter figures being appreciably better than the previous Anglia could manage, indicating a much improved open-road overtaking ability. A mean maximum speed of 76.8mph with a best one-way 79mph had been recorded, and the overall fuel consumption during the inevitably hard-driven test mileage was 36.1mpg, although 41mpg had resulted 'on one fairly brisk run with four people on board and using 60mph as a natural crusing speed'. *The Autocar* concluded: 'In terms of speed and acceleration the new Anglia is one of the fastest four-seater British cars of under 1,000cc engine capacity, and with this and its other attributes there seems little doubt that it will not be long before we see it appearing in competitive events, no doubt with some measure of success. More important is its appeal as a compact family car which is both pleasant to travel in and to drive. With its willing engine, its light and well planned controls, and the high standard of comfort and finish provided, it will undoubtedly answer these requirements excellently.'

At the Earls Court Motor Show in October, the Anglia was, of course, one of the star attractions, although it did have to share the limelight in the

The top model was identified by 'Super' badges on the bonnet and on the rear quarter pillar.

small-car class with the BMC Mini and the Triumph Herald, which were also making their Earls Court debut that year. Both these rivals were considered by many to be technically more interesting than the new Anglia, which was indeed of very conventional layout, quite unlike the transverse-engined Mini with its rubber cone suspension, or the Herald, which was built on a separate chassis and also offered independent suspension all round.

Conventional in layout the Anglia may well have been, but its power unit was far in advance of any rivals, whilst its MacPherson-strut front suspension was still unique to Ford at that time. In addition to the wide following it was to gain at home, those discerning buyers from overseas were ordering new Anglias at an unprecedented rate. By the time the Earls

Chrome trim strips bordered the Super's contrasting side stripe. The direction indicator is in the upper part of the rear light assembly.

Court display closed on October 31, export orders for the 105E, including those placed in the pre-launch period, had totalled 101,000 cars, 66,000 of which were destined for North America, following what had been Dagenham's most successful new car launch up to that time.

Demand in fact proved very hard to meet, and early in 1960 arrangements were made between Dagenham and Ford Belgium for the latter to assemble 500 Anglias a month at their Antwerp plant, whilst Ford Australia had to double its original 1960 estimates after the entire stock of Anglias there and in New Zealand were sold out within two days of the model's local announcement.

Teething troubles were remarkably few. Some early examples did suffer from leaks when water thrown up by the front wheels entered the car, but an early production modification was introduced which cured this. More

91

An Anglia Super with whitewall tyres. The wheeltrims on this car are those introduced with the Mk 3 Zodiac, whereas the Super illustrated earlier has 109E Classic wheeltrims.

serious was a complaint from some owners of a definite flat spot in the carburation, and modifications to the carburettor were introduced in January 1960, which, unfortunately, did not always effect a complete cure. This particular problem, which manifested itself only at low rpm, was no doubt magnified somewhat by the Anglia's combination of high overall gearing with such a free-revving engine not designed with much emphasis on low-speed pulling power — quite a change from its sidevalve predecessors — and therefore it troubled less those who used the gearbox freely. Not all cars were affected, and the Anglia had no trouble at all in establishing itself as Britain's number-one selling car in 1960; 200,000 sales in the first year were certainly cause for celebration, a long-distance endurance test was planned — of which more in a later chapter — and a nationwide Anglia Birthday Treasure Hunt for new Anglia owners was organized in conjunction with Ford dealers. Area winners contested a national final on Sunday, October 16, 1960, which resulted in Mr T. Picken, of Birmingham, winning the first prize of £500, with Mr D.Conway, of Norwich, and Mr T. Oldham, of Nottingham, claiming the second and third prizes of £300 and £200. The prizegiving was at Earls Court the following Saturday, and the prizewinners were invited to dinner and the theatre in London as guests of the Ford Motor Company on the Friday evening, with overnight hotel accommodation provided.

At Earls Court in 1960, the Anglia shared the top spot on the Ford stand with a Zodiac, the two cars projecting the 'two-car family' theme in quite spectacular fashion, being painted in white with all bright.metal parts inside and out in 22-carat gold plate. This involved 306 separate items, including the tyre valve caps, on the Anglia, and 542 parts on the Zodiac. The interiors were upholstered in white hide edged in black and embossed with gold stars. At that time, only 2% of car-owning families in Britain possessed more than one car, but Ford estimated that this figure would treble over the next 10 years, by which time some 300,000 households would have a second car.

Small changes phased-in during 1961 were an improved water pump gland to cure squeaks which sometimes emanated from that component, a new fuel pump incorporating a sediment bowl, and a mechanical timing chain tensioner. A smoothly-styled estate car joined the range in time for the 1961 motor show, available in both basic and De Luxe forms at £679 and £701 respectively. Exactly similar to the saloon, inside and out, from the centre pillar forward, and on the same 7ft 6½in wheelbase, the estate car's rear end increased the overall length by an inch to 12ft 10½in. The new rear bodywork was styled by Canadian Roy Brown, of Edsel fame, the 105E estate being his first project since taking over as head of styling at Dagenham after having transferred from Ford of America, where he had worked since 1951. Blending in neatly with the Anglia's front end treatment, the estate bodywork offered a maximum 35cu ft of luggage space over a completely flat, 54in long floor with the rear seat squab folded. On the De Luxe the rear floor area was covered in heavy-duty linoleum with alloy rubbing strips, whereas the standard model had a painted wooden floor. The entire area, including the wheelarches, was fully trimmed, and the car-style roof lining continued to the rear. The full-width tailgate, hinged at the top, extended down to floor level; it was fully counterbalanced. An inconvenience, though, was that the rear floor section had to be lifted to remove the spare wheel, which now resided horizontally beneath the loading area — an easy enough task in itself, but requiring the removal of any items being carried. Mechanical changes were confined to a lower axle ratio of 4.444:1, and stiffer rear springs consisting of seven leaves rather than the saloon's four. Slightly larger-section tyres — 5.60 x 13 — were also fitted in anticipation of increased loads, and gave overall gearing of 15.3mph/1,000rpm in conjunction with the lower final-drive ratio.

Substantially built, the estate car weighed unladen almost 1cwt more than the saloon, and when tested by *The Autocar* (May 18, 1962) a slight performance decrease was evident. Acceleration from rest to 50 and 60mph was accomplished in 20.1 and 36.4 seconds respectively, and the

A De Luxe estate car displaying a whole collection of additional equipment. The spot and fog lamps, overriders, hubcap medallions, nearside wing mirror, exhaust deflector and whitewall tyres were all Ford-listed options and accessories.

Introduced at the 1964 Turin
Motor Show, the Anglia Torino
had an extensively reworked
body styled by Michelotti. Much
of the original Anglia centre
section and almost everything
under the skin remained
unchanged, and new front and
rear panelwork was manu-
factured in Italy. Both 997cc and
1,198cc engines were offered,
the latter coming complete with
a Weber carburettor and
earning a car so equipped the
title 'Torino S'. The former head
of Ford International, Filmer
Paradise, had much to do with
the development and was
presented with a silver-painted
example by grateful Italian Ford
dealers. Another surviving
example (bottom) was
photographed recently at its
Luxembourg home.

mean maximum speed was 71.7mph. Speeds of 23mph, 39mph and 65mph in the three lower gears all corresponded to more than 6,000rpm, and *The Autocar* commented: 'The engine is certainly one of the smoothest and quietest small car power units in current production, but it is one which is intended to be worked vigorously, with ample revs in hand. The man who expects to slog along with the Anglia always in top gear will be disappointed; but with intelligent use of the gearbox to keep the engine always revving briskly, the delightful smoothness and eagerness of the unit are appreciated.'

The stiffer rear suspension seemed to have improved the handling qualities, *The Autocar* noting that: 'When cornering, saloon versions of the Anglia have a tendency to hop at the rear on a rough surface. The stronger rear springs and slight extra weight have made this characteristic less noticeable, and it was generally considered that the estate car handled appreciably better than the saloon....Taken to the limits of cornering, the tail end begins to slide outwards without any sudden breakaway, and balances the basic understeer....With only the driver on board, the ride is firm, and there is some tendency for the car to give a rather bouncy ride at the rear....Four adults on board took much of the bounciness out of the suspension, and with either the full complement of passengers or the test load of concrete blocks in the rear, the car still handled unexpectedly well. On corners, in this condition, there was no excessive oversteer, and directional stability remained good.'

Some criticism was levelled at comfort: despite the fact that rearward movement of the driver's seat had been increased, it was thought that an

Anglia control layout. A black steering wheel became standard on all but Super models late in 1964.

unduly 'knees bent' attitude was still forced upon the driver. Referring to the increased cost by comparison with the saloon, *The Autocar* concluded: 'This is an increase in the region of 10% of the total sum to be paid, and no doubt many will consider that the extra is fully justified by the increased accommodation, dual-purpose nature, and by the different appearance. It is certainly a sturdy and practically designed car.' Those ordering an Anglia saloon now could specify the 4.444:1 axle ratio as a no-cost option.

Troubles were still being experienced by some owners with the carburation, and *The Autocar* had commented on this in their estate car test report. However, a new Solex carburettor incorporating an accelerator pump was soon to become part of the Anglia's specification, and this finally cured the flat-spot problem. Owners of existing Anglias still troubled by this could fit the new carburettor, available as a replacement item at £9 15s.

The range was further extended in October 1962 with the introduction of the Anglia Super, which, in addition to having greater power, was also trimmed and equipped usefully beyond the De Luxe standards. Recognizable externally by two-tone paintwork in which a contrasting colour was applied both to a full-length 'flash' along the sides of the car and to the roof panel, the Super also came with elegant anodized aluminium wheeltrim rings. Standard equipment over the normal De Luxe included the heater unit, a windscreen washer and a cigar lighter. Fitted carpets replaced the cheaper car's rubber floor covering, and a full-width padded top to the facia was a useful safety feature. The PVC upholstery had a 'metallic' looking finish, and both rear seat passengers were provided with easily reached grab straps on the centre pillars.

A steering wheel colour-keyed to match the rest of the interior became a feature of the Super in October 1964. At the same time it became possible to specify a Super-style trim package as an extra-cost option on the 997cc De Luxe car, as shown here.

Separate amber flashing indicators and white sidelamps replaced the original combined units at the front in September 1965.

The extra power was provided by the 1,198cc engine, which had appeared in the new Cortina model announced at the end of September and came complete with that car's excellent all-synchromesh gearbox. The extra capacity, of course, was achieved by the adoption of a longer stroke, with a new, slightly longer-throw crankshaft — still hollowed out — increasing the measurement to 58.17mm. On a slightly lower compression ratio of 8.7:1, but still with a similar Solex accelerator pump type carburettor, the 1,198cc engine gave 48.5bhp at 4,800rpm and produced 65lb/ft torque at the same 2,700rpm as on the smaller unit. The Cortina's wider brake drums, with shoes giving 81.7sq in lining area, were also part of the Super specification. A purchase tax reduction earlier in the year and a basic price cut by Ford had brought the Standard and De Luxe Anglias down to £514 and £538 respectively, with the Super now completing the line-up at £598.

The Motor soon put an Anglia Super through its paces (R/T No 48/62), describing it as a 'refined and faster version of Dagenham's most successful car'. Pointing out that it was '...laid out on what may be termed conventional lines', *The Motor* nevertheless thought that: 'Its orthodoxy is of a highly developed kind, however, which results in an exceptionally smooth and unfatiguing motor car with good handling.' The performance showed a substantial improvement, *The Motor* recording times of 21.6 and 34.9 seconds from rest to 60 and 70mph respectively, and a mean maximum speed of 81.8mph. The overall fuel consumption for the 1,619 miles test was 33mpg, and at a constant 70mph cruise the Anglia Super would return 30.5mpg. Good news for Anglia buyers who wished for the enhanced performance without the Super's more lavish trim and equipment level was that a '1200' package which consisted of the 1,198cc engine, all-synchromesh gearbox and larger brakes, was to be available on the cheaper Anglias for just £24 extra.

Two views of a 1966 model Anglia Super. The Ford badge behind the wheelarch on the nearside front wing is now in an oval setting rather than the earlier oblong.

In July 1960, after months of surveying and soil investigation, foundation work had begun at Ford's 362-acre site at Halewood, on Merseyside. The first stage was the construction of a £28-million factory of 2,600,000sq ft in which all body manufacturing operations from stamping out panels to final assembly could be undertaken, whilst engines, transmissions, etc, would still be supplied by Dagenham. Stage two was a much longer term projection, in which it was intended almost to double the factory area and include a foundry and manufacturing facilities for mechanical components.

Stage one was completed early in 1963, and Anglia assembly was transferred there, the first car, a De Luxe model, being registered 1KF on March 6 that year. This particular Anglia survives today, on display in Liverpool's museum, having been presented to the City of Liverpool by the Ford Motor Company in 1969. Its former registration number, however, is now used on Liverpool's mayoral limousine.

By this time, the Anglia had lost its top-selling spot: its Ford stablemate, the new Cortina, and the recently introduced BMC Austin/Morris 1100 series were now fighting it out at the top of the sales league. Nevertheless, the Anglia remained extremely popular with both the family man and the transport managers of large concerns to whom the model was giving remarkable service. Kraft Foods had a fleet of 250 Anglias which were covering a total of $6\frac{1}{4}$-million miles a year, whilst the Anglias belonging to Birds Eye Foods were each travelling 22,000 miles a year — an 8-million mile total — at an overall fleet average of 37.5mpg and a $\frac{1}{2}$d per mile service/repair/replacements/valeting cost. Other well-known companies using Anglias were J. Lyons & Co Ltd (Lyons Maid), W. Moorhouse Ltd (Moorhouse jams), and building contractors George Wimpey & Co Ltd, whose transport fleet included 240 Anglias changed on a three-year basis.

On February 4, 1964, Ford announced a substantial price-cut on the entire Anglia range, amounting to no less than £36 on the basic model and

The Thames van derivative of the 105E first appeared in 1961 and was available in 5cwt and 7cwt De Luxe forms, the latter having rather less-basic trim and some extra chrome embellishments. The passenger seat was an extra in either case! Model designation was 307E with the 997cc engine, 309E if the optional 1,198cc unit was fitted. 'Thames' was dropped in March 1965, after which the vehicle became the Anglia Van. The curved bottom edge of the side doors allowed full opening when parked on a cambered road with a high kerb.

made possible by great improvements in production facilities, a figure close to £100 million having been spent over the previous three years on the most modern plant and equipment. Prices now of £478, £510 and £575 for the basic, De Luxe and Super respectively, compared very favourably with those of the Austin A40 Farina at £556 (basic) and £599 (De Luxe) and the two-door Morris Minor at £515 and £540 in its basic and De Luxe configurations. Indeed, undercutting the Anglia was only the BMC Mini which, as is now well known, was losing money, whereas the Anglia, even at its new low prices, was estimated to be making Ford a profit in the region of £45 per car. Commenting on the price reductions, Ford's Managing Director, Mr Allen Barke, exclaimed: 'The Anglia is now a better car than ever and is accepted throughout the world as Britain's most reliable light car. It has consistently exceeded our sales targets — current production is 600 a day — and it is headed for its first million.'

The Anglias on the Ford stand at Earls Court in October 1964 displayed several cosmetic changes, with both the De Luxe and Super models now featuring interior paintwork colour-keyed to the trim rather than the car's exterior colour. A black finish was adopted for the switches, controls and steering wheel on the standard and De Luxe cars, whilst the Super now also boasted a colour-keyed steering wheel. A big improvement was the provision in the facia of all models for a built-in radio, allowing it to blend in harmoniously with its surroundings. A new range of cloth trim was also available at extra cost throughout the range, whilst the Super's normal seat trim was in a new knitweave PVC which 'breathed', and was said to offer more comfort than the usual PVC-coated fabrics. The previous '1200' package consisting principally of the larger engine was now deleted as a De Luxe option, but there was a Super package with the Super's more expensive interior trim, and complete with the contrasting colour side-flash and its associated chrome mouldings. At a modest £25 extra, this was excellent value for those wishing for rather more luxury without the extra power of the top-of-the-range model. On the safety side of things, a welcome fitting on the more expensive versions was the standardization of windscreen washers, and all models now featured seat belt mounting

Nothing if not versatile! This Anglia owned by a cattle-breeding centre has a modified boot lid to accommodate outsize churns.

points. Just one mechanical change was evident, this being a more efficient radiator of the modine type in which the conventional arrangement of several rows of finned tubes was replaced by a single row of much deeper tubes.

Demand for the Anglia had risen considerably more than anticipated since the price-cut earlier in the year, to such an extent that the production capacity at Halewood had been completely outstripped, and a supplementary assembly programme was introduced at Dagenham in order to bring output up to the 700 per day which was now necessary to keep pace with the market's requirements.

Many saloon buyers were now specifying the optional lower gearing, apparently considering the increase in acceleration which this provided well worth the small sacrifice in the ultimate speed potential. As this trend continued to increase during 1965 it was decided to standardize the 4.444:1 ratio, with the original 4.125:1 now becoming the option. *The Motor* published a full road test report of the lower-geared saloon late in the year (R/T No 43/65), noting that: 'The Anglia, tested in De Luxe form, has aged remarkably little in its six years and its very conventionality is probably one of its better selling points, coupled as it must be after such an interval with a reputation for good, reliable service.' A maximum speed of 73.3mph was accompanied by acceleration which allowed 50 and 60mph to be reached from rest in 15.6 and 26.2 seconds respectively, figures sufficient to indicate that the Anglia was still very competitive in this department in the small car class. Overall fuel consumption seemed rather high at 29.5mpg, but this was explained as being the result of much mileage

An Anglia on the beat. Many police forces equipped their former foot-patrol men with Anglia 'panda cars' during the 1960s.

in London traffic in addition to some fast motorway journeys, and *The Motor*'s calculated touring consumption was a more respectable 39.9mpg. The handling came in for considerable praise with the comments: 'If the Anglia is beginning to show its age at all it is in the narrow, top-heavy feel of the car as you sit in it for the first time; this is purely an illusion and it handles very well.... Most of the time it hovers safely between neutral and understeer — understeer on fast corners when it stays fairly flat, and neutral on tighter ones as the roll angle increases. The roll is only ever really noticeable when you are squealing round tight corners. The final limit cornering characteristic is oversteer, although it is difficult to tell whether the reduction of lock is to correct oversteer or to compensate for the gradual loss of understeer as speed is scrubbed off by the front tyres....This detailed handling analysis for what is essentially a family car, shows that the Anglia is entirely safe in emergencies.' The Anglia was fitted with the recently introduced Goodyear G8 tyres, and *The Motor* reported: '...with the improved tyres it is difficult to promote tail slides in the wet. These tyres have certainly closed the gap between wet and dry handling.' Some criticism was, however, aimed at the car in respect of ride comfort, because suspension which gave good handling was '...not usually the best arrangement for a comfortable ride.... The Anglia conforms to the Ford pattern, combining good handling with the ability to take heavy loads without getting too near the bump stops, but the ride is still rather lively.... On new, well-surfaced roads this is not a worrying feature, but roadmakers' humps and hollows on other roads can be uncomfortable.' Overall, though, this was quite a complimentary report on an inexpensive car which remained virtually unaltered after six years in production, and yet in general terms could hold its own very well indeed amongst small cars at a time when so-called advanced engineering was being widely applied by other manufacturers in the field.

Continuing in great demand for business and private users alike, the Anglia was also joining forces with its larger stablemate, the Zephyr 6, in the fight to uphold the law, 58 Anglias having been recruited by the Lancashire Constabulary in the summer of 1965. Painted lagoon blue with white doors, they quickly became known locally as the 'Blue Bonnets', and were manned by former foot-patrol officers — the once familiar 'bobby on the beat'. After their first nine months service, in April 1966, it was announced by Lancashire's Chief Constable, Colonel T.E.S. Johnston, CBE, that reported crime in the areas covered by the Anglias had fallen by 31%, cases of damage were down by 53%, whilst traffic accidents had been reduced by 16%. This success resulted in many more police forces equipping their beat-men with what became widely known as 'Panda' cars during 1966, many of which were Anglias, including 24 purchased by Scotland Yard.

Meanwhile, since January 1966, Anglias equipped with the 997cc engine had been fitted with a new Ford downdraught carburettor and a Ford distributor in place of the previous Solex and Lucas components, changes which did not affect the quoted power outputs. The millionth Anglia was due to leave the production line in September, and a nationwide contest to find the 'Best kept Anglia in Britain' was organized to celebrate the event. A total of £5,000 in prize money was being offered, and although the competition was to celebrate a million Anglia saloons and estates there was also a category for the Anglia-derived 5cwt and 7cwt Thames vans. Local competitions organized by the dealerships took place between August 5 and September 3, with the winners proceeding to area finals on September 12 and the area finalists going forward to the grand final at the company's headquarters at Brentwood, in Essex, on September 25. The vehicles entered were divided into three categories according to mileage, and the outright winners in both the car and van classes were high-mileage examples. The best kept car was a 1961 model owned by Mr A. Sandford, of Merioneth, in Wales, who ran a local driving school. After 188,000 miles, during which a total of 386 'L' drivers had taken lessons in the car, Mr Sandford's Anglia was still running well on the original engine and gearbox, the engine in fact not ever having had the cylinder head removed in that time. The best van was judged to be that entered by Mr L. Chesham of Westcliff-on-Sea, Essex, his 1962 Thames 5cwt having covered 116,000 miles on its original engine and transmission. £250 each was presented to the winners by actor Brian Blessed — then well-known as Fancy Smith of Z Cars fame on BBC TV — with smaller cash prizes going to 28 other competitors.

Production of the Anglia range continued for a further year, during which the Super models were available in Venetian Gold or Blue Mink metallic paint finishes with black interior trim. Production ceased in November 1967, the Anglia making way for a newcomer in the form of a European, rather than British, small Ford to be known as the Escort. All-new it may have been called, and new in many ways it was, but the Escort was also recognizably an evolution of the Anglia concept, no radical departure proving necessary from that successful formula.

CHAPTER 6

Anglia and the tuners

Modifying the 105E

Throughout its lengthy production run, and for some considerable time after, enthusiasts wishing for a more potent 105E had an almost bewildering array of performance equipment from which to choose. One of the earliest conversions on offer was provided by Arden Racing & Sportscars, and consisted of both engine and suspension modifications at an all-inclusive fitted price of £67 16s. Cylinder head work consisted of raised compression ratio, polished ports and the installation of stronger valve springs. In addition, there were twin $1\frac{1}{4}$-inch SU carburettors on a new combined inlet and exhaust manifold, and a straight-through silencer. A second anti-roll bar, which could be purchased separately if required for just £3 10s, was clamped to the original, thus considerably stiffening up the front suspension. *The Motor* reported on the Arden Anglia in their issue of May 4, 1960: 'Having a perfectly standard Anglia on the strength of staff cars we were able to drive modified and unmodified versions in quick succession, thus providing an interesting comparison. The extra urge was very useful in what is a somewhat over-geared car and makes using the gearbox a real pleasure by way of the dividends that it pays, over 70mph being usefully available in third gear, whilst the 4.1 top allows comparatively high cruising speeds and gives the modified car a remarkably good "best one way" maximum. Flat spots in the carburation have not been entirely eliminated, however, and a curious effect is that at certain points in the rev range, maximum acceleration is not achieved by maximum depression of the accelerator pedal. With its extra urge at high rpm the "souped up" engine uses more fuel than do untuned examples.'

The Arden Anglia had accelerated to 70mph from rest in 32.3 seconds, and continued to a creditable mean maximum speed of 80.6mph with a best one-way time equalling 87mph. The fuel consumption had indeed suffered, an overall 27.0mpg being recorded for what had been a hard-driven test. In respect of the extra anti-roll bar, *The Motor* commented very favourably, noting that it was '... extremely effective and so improved the general road behaviour of the car that the member of our staff who normally drives an Anglia at once ordered one, feeling that it was a worthwhile addition even on an untuned car. Not only did it improve the cornering power sufficiently to embarrass at least one well-known make of sports car which we met on our journeyings, but directional stability was also improved on the straight.'

105

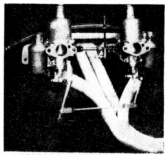

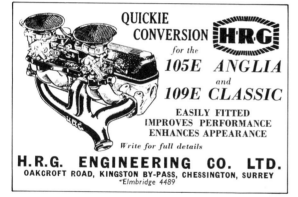
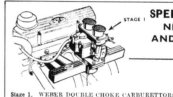
A wide variety of performance equipment became available for the 105E Anglia, as these contemporary advertisements show, so that an Anglia could be developed into a distinctly sporting motor car tailored to suit its owner's needs. It also made life more exciting for the increasing number of specials and limited-production sports cars using the Ford power unit.

A similar conversion to that from Arden was available from Rally Equipment, whose modified cylinder head, with a compression ratio of 9.2:1, had the additional advantage of bigger valves. Twin $1\frac{1}{4}$-inch SUs again supplied the mixture, and included in the £55 10s being asked was a new rocker-box cover with polished cooling fins. All of this enabled the Anglia to reach 90mph, and accelerate from rest to 70mph in rather less time than the standard model required to reach 60. For a further £8 15s Rally Equipment could supply a pair of trailing-link suspension arms, which kept the Anglia's rear wheels firmly on the road by preventing spring wind-up during hard acceleration.

An interesting alternative to the twin-carburettor installations available, offering a broadly similar improvement, was the GM Carburettor Company's single Weber carburettor conversion at £55, for which the Weber came complete with a combined inlet and four-branch exhaust manifold. A less expensive single-carburettor conversion, which nevertheless included a modified cylinder head, was also available from the same company at £33. The carburation in this case was by an accelerator-pump type Solex and with this conversion an Anglia could reach 70mph from rest in 36 seconds whilst on its way to a genuine 80mph maximum. An accelerator-pump type Solex on a curved four-branch induction manifold was also the basis of Wilen Engineering's low-cost Anglia conversion. No cylinder head work was involved in this instance; instead, a modified camshaft was fitted which gave particularly good results at the top end of the range, although at the expense of bottom-end flexibility. With the original carburettor and camshaft being taken in exchange the Wilen conversion was good value in component form for the home mechanic at £27 10s: professional fitting, however, was £10 extra.

The success of modifications such as these prompted the Ford Motor Company to offer a Performance Plus conversion for the Anglia which could be specified when ordering a new car, on which, of course, it did not invalidate the manufacturer's warranty as tuning equipment from other sources usually did. Featuring a larger, 25mm Solex carburettor and air filter, a new camshaft, stronger valve springs, gaskets, etc, and, interestingly, a set of heavy-duty main bearing shells, the package was very good value at £13. Considerable dismantling of the engine was necessary, and when fitted retrospectively at a Ford agency there was an £11 10s fitting charge, which did, however, include decarbonizing and valve grinding. Although giving a useful improvement in acceleration,

particularly in conjunction with the 4.444:1 axle ratio, the Performance Plus conversion showed no gains in maximum speed irrespective of which axle was employed. It did make the engine appreciably more flexible than the standard unit, usefully smoothing out the power delivery at the bottom end of the rev range and eliminating the flat-spot which plagued many early Anglias.

At the opposite end of the scale, for £240 the Anglia owner could purchase a Cosworth conversion consisting of an extensively reworked cylinder head, twin Weber carburettors and a special camshaft. This enabled an Anglia to reach 80mph from rest in 30 seconds whilst on its way to a genuine 100mph maximum. With little power developed below 4,000rpm, however, this conversion was more suited to competition work than ordinary road use.

There was, too, an alternative approach to improving performance. By avoiding the complication of multi-carburettor installations and their attendant tuning problems, and not requiring the engine rebuilding needed with reworked cylinder heads, new camshafts and so on, supercharging

Allard and Super Speed were leading suppliers of Anglia tuning equipment. Both firms were engaged in motor sport and both were able to provide a complete modified car if required. Supercharger installation was a particular speciality of Allard's.

was an attractive way of achieving substantially enhanced power outputs from a standard engine. Also, because it was bolted onto an unmodified engine, the supercharger could easily be removed if it became desirable to revert to standard specification, something not possible with other conversions in which components had been taken in exchange. Forced induction resulted in measurable improvements at the bottom of the rpm range, so endowing the car with increased flexibility, in addition to the more spectacular gains evident at the top end. A vane-type Shorrock supercharger for the Anglia was available as a kit at £69 15s or fitted for £75, from Sydney Allard. This installation enabled a 997cc Anglia to reach 70mph from rest in 27 seconds and continue to almost 90mph, whilst also allowing the car to progress smoothly from 20 to 40mph in a creditable 12 seconds on the high top gear ratio of 4.125:1. Fuel consumption figures for constant-speed running within the Anglia's normal performance range would be similar to the standard car, but full use of the extra performance — which, as can be seen from the figures quoted, would certainly not have disgraced a 2-litre saloon in 1961 — would result in an overall consumption of around 23mpg. In addition to being a well-known competition motorist, Sydney Allard also ran a Ford dealership and therefore could supply a new Anglia ready equipped with the supercharger. With further modifications, at an all-inclusive price of £750, the car became an Anglia Allardette.

Export rear springs and an additional front anti-roll bar clamped to the original, Dunlop front disc brakes, a recalibrated speedometer reading to 105mph, and a wood-rimmed steering wheel were all features of the Allardette, which could be recognized externally by its chromed badges at the front and rear. Ford wheeltrims and hubcap medallions were also standard Allardette fittings, whilst a range of optional extras included a rev-counter and other instrumentation in a supplementary dash panel, safety belts and a plastic stick-on number-plate. With the latter item fixed on the sloping bonnet top just above the grille, twin oblong foglamps were mounted centrally beneath the bumper bar in the space vacated by the normal number-plate. So equipped, an Anglia became an excellent sports saloon, with road manners quite in keeping with its 90mph capability, whilst at the other end of the scale the improvement in tractability served to enhance its compact, about-town role.

The Allardette name was applied to other variations on the Anglia theme by Sydney Allard, the next in the series being the Allardette 109. Rather than the supercharged 997cc power unit, this car, which appeared late in 1961, had the increased-capacity motor (1,340cc) from the newly introduced Ford Classic, which carried the Ford designation 109E. As the larger Classic also featured Girling front disc brakes, these became the normal Allardette equipment in place of those previously provided by Dunlop. An example in this configuration, priced at £740, was tested by *Autocar,* their report appearing in the issue of March 9, 1962, in which the test staff noted: 'No special tuning is done on the Classic engine. Compared with the Anglia unit, however, maximum power and torque are increased by 38.5% and 41% respectively. It is no surprise, therefore, to find that the Allardette has a very lively and effortless performance. Perhaps the first thing one notices about driving this car is the very small throttle opening needed for acceleration in town and for cruising at up to 60-65mph.... Except for town work and when maximum performance is required, the Allardette can be treated virtually as a top-gear car. It will pull away strongly although not very smoothly in this ratio from 25mph and, as speed builds up, the acceleration is so good that it seems hardly necessary to use third gear. This is in sharp contrast to the behaviour of the standard Anglia, which demands very full use of the gearbox.'

Criticism was levelled at the engine with comments such as: 'This engine did not seem to like revving hard, when it became harsh and rather noisy,

Two big twin-choke Weber carburettors fill most of the available space in the engine compartment of a Super Speed modified Anglia. Those unfiltered air intakes must have been fairly noisy!

and there appeared to be little benefit from making it do so.' Nevertheless, *Autocar* pointed out: 'Overall, the performance is substantially better than that of the Anglia.... To 60 and 70mph from rest, the acceleration times are 8.3sec and 16.7sec better... and top gear acceleration is greatly improved....' The matter of the 1,340cc unit's unwillingness to rev hard, coupled with the fact that the overall gearing remained unchanged, resulted in a maximum speed better by only 3mph or so, despite the availability of some 15bhp extra. The 1,340cc version of the '80 bore' series of Ford engines did, in fact, earn a poor reputation in this respect by comparison with the other units in the range, and in its Allardette installation both maximum speed and through-the-gears acceleration were actually slightly inferior to the 1,198cc Anglias introduced sometime later by Ford themselves. Top gear acceleration, however, greatly improved throughout the range, with the times taken to go from 20 to 40mph and from 40 to 60mph of 9.9 seconds and 12.6 seconds respectively, showing marked superiority over the standard Anglia's 14.4 seconds and 20.4 seconds. The suspension modifications had, according to *Autocar*: '...made the ride firmer, though not uncomfortable', and it was also observed that: '...there is more resistance to roll during fast cornering, giving a stronger sense of stability.'

With the introduction of the 1,500cc five-bearing engine in 1962 for larger Ford models, a very effective transplant became possible. In fact, at one stage, Ford themselves considered marketing an Anglia 1500 which was to have incorporated suspension modifications by noted saloon car racing driver Alan Mann. Exactly why the project was dropped is not clear, but at least one prototype was completed by Mann, and survived for some years in the hands of a Ford employee.

Naturally enough, Allard was soon offering a range of Allardette 1500s, with the basic 1500GT, at £737, featuring the new engine alone, tuned in this instance to produce 85bhp at 5,800rpm. This was sufficient to propel the Anglia at 97mph, and enable it to accelerate from rest to 70mph in an excellent 17.9 seconds. With this performance it was desirable to purchase the other established Allardette features which, with the addition now of rear axle anti-tramp bars and suspension lowered by 2 inches all round, were available as a package deal on the 1500GT for an extra £59. A wide variety of optional equipment — a large-bore exhaust system (£15 10s), wider wheels with 165 x 13 radial tyres (£56), 3.9:1 rear axle (£23) and adjustable rear shock absorbers (£19 10s) — were available to choice. Specifying all these, plus a Shorrock supercharger, resulted in an Allardette 1500GTS, which would accelerate from rest to 50mph in just 8.2 seconds and to 70mph in 11.7 seconds whilst heading for a maximum speed of more than 115mph.

Any of the Allard equipment could be purchased separately — the disc brakes, for instance, at £39, or the anti-tramp bars at £3 18s 6d the pair — so that an Anglia owner could tailor his car to suit his own requirements exactly, for either competition or fast road work. Naturally enough, some individuals combined Allard bits with engine conversions and accessories from different companies. Nobody knows precisely how many Anglias ended up tuned or modified to some degree, but there was certainly no shortage of available parts, large or small, for the job.

CHAPTER 7

Anglia in competition

Racing, rallying and record-breaking

The new Anglia made its international rallying debut little more than a month after its announcement, with a strong works entry contesting the RAC International Rally in November 1959 alongside the Mk2 Zephyrs. Cuth Harrison and Denis Scott were each at the wheel of a new Anglia, as were Anne Hall and Mary Wright, the latter, with two Ladies Cups to her credit in the East African Safari, having been flown in from Nairobi by the Ford Motor Company specially for this event. Mary Wright's rally, however, came to a very premature end as, not long after leaving the Blackpool start, her Anglia mounted a bank and overturned in one of the narrow Lake District lanes. In contrast, Anne Hall had an excellent run, despite conditions of fog and snow which eliminated many contestants, and at the finish, her Anglia was the highest placed of the new Fords, in 20th place, a position which earned her the Ladies Cup in this important event.

Three works Anglias were amongst the entries in the 1960 Monte Carlo Rally, with those of Anne Hall and Graham Hill running in the standard category, whilst the Ian Walker/Gerry Burgess car was entered in the modified class. A twin-choke Solex carburettor on a redesigned inlet manifold, combined with enlarged valve porting, raised the 997cc engine's output to 52bhp, with export rear suspension and an additional 6-gallon fuel tank completing the modifications. All three cars were running with Dunlop Duraband tyres on the front wheels and Dunlop Weathermasters on the rear, with two tungsten-studded Durabands carried as spares for use on the rear should icebound conditions be encountered.

The modified Anglia proved unsuitable due to the fact that it developed little power at all at low rpm, and had difficulty in maintaining the 'modified' schedule even on reasonably clear sections. Remembering this, Gerry Burgess recently recalled: 'There can never have been a rally car so mistakenly set up as that one. It would literally not pull its own weight with less than 3,500 revs, and so failed to climb the first really icy slope!' The other two Anglias, however, fared much better, Anne Hall going particularly well in the foggy conditions encountered early on, and arriving at Chambéry unpenalized and in the lead for the Ladies Cup. Graham Hill, too, was well-placed here, in spite of a dynamo failure which had cost the Anglia the use of its lamps and windscreen wipers. The route from Chambéry to Monaco was a regularity test split up into five sections, and several icebound passes ensured that few competitors remained penalty-

Success the first time out: Anne Hall on her way to winning the Ladies' Cup in the 1959 RAC Rally, the 105E's first international event. Here, Anne corners hard during a special test in the wet at Aintree.

free. Nevertheless, the two standard Anglias arrived at Monte Carlo sufficiently well-placed to qualify for the final mountain circuit stage in the Alpes Maritimes.

Unfortunately, snatching brakes on his Anglia caused Graham Hill to retire, and Anne Hall, too, ran into trouble. 'I thought the steering was a bit odd, but we continued to belt on for a while', she recalled recently. Fortunately, however, Anne decided to investigate, and discovered one front wheel held on by just one nut, and that only finger-tight. The slight delay cost her the lead in the Ladies Cup, Pat Moss taking that honour with her Austin A40, finishing a creditable 17th overall, whilst Anne brought the Anglia in to the finish in 36th place.

The next major event was the East African Safari, and in addition to the Zephyrs that year there was the first works-entered Anglia team. The 84 starters, including 14 nominated teams, left Nairobi to tackle the 1,900-miles southern loop through Tanganyika. Few cars remained unpenalized for very long, and on the first tight section, a 26-miles stage to be covered at a 52mph average, the Anglias of Peter Hughes and Jeff Uren both lost time, putting them behind the Auto Union (DKW) 1000s which were strongly fancied contenders in this class. However, the leading Auto Union went out soon after with engine trouble. Apart from tearing off their exhaust systems on the rutted and rock-strewn tracks, the Anglias continued to go well, although Jeff Uren's car did side-swipe a large boulder, which jammed the driver's door for the remainder of the event.

At Dar es Salaam, 1,000 miles from Nairobi, there was a welcome hour-long rest stop, but 15 of the starters did not even make it that far. The route turned north again back to Nairobi over more unmade sections, and the pace required to keep time now really began to take its toll. Four of the six works Sunbeam Rapiers retired, as did three of the four BMC Minis, and with others dropping out regularly there were only four of the nominated teams intact when the survivors reached Nairobi for a well-earned night's rest before attempting the northern loop. The teams still intact were Mercedes 190, Zephyr, Volkswagen, and Anglia, in that order: in addition there were several individual cars still in action, including a lone Auto Union, which was holding a narrow lead over the Anglias in their class.

Soon after leaving Nairobi for the north, one of the remaining Volkswagens went out after overturning, leaving just two of the original seven which had started, and a lengthy stop for repairs by the lone Auto Union handed the class lead to the Anglias, which were still going well, although their crews had now apparently given up replacing silencers and tailpipes. The 1,200-miles northern loop eliminated many of the remainder, including all the surviving British cars (Standard Vanguards, Sunbeam Rapiers, Austin Cambridges, a Triumph Herald, a Morris Oxford, a Jaguar and the BMC Minis) apart from the Anglia and Zephyr teams and a lone Hillman Minx. Only 25 of the original 84 starters finished the course, all four Anglias entered surviving to take first, second, third and fifth places in their class.

Amongst the celebrations arranged by Ford for the 105E model's first birthday, in September 1960, was an endurance run in which Anglias were to aim to cover 10,000 miles in seven days and nights. Three Anglias were to make the attempt at the Goodwood circuit, each car being driven by a team of three drivers, a racing driver, a Ford agent, and a motoring journalist. The cars were to be strictly standard models in respect of all mechanical elements and running gear, and the run was to be observed by the RAC, although any records broken would not in fact be officially recognized as it was intended that repairs would be carried out on the cars if necessary during the course of the week, with replacement parts being

Ford line-up at the end of the 1960 East African Safari Rally. The Zephyrs won the team prize and the Anglias won their class — altogether an impressive performance.

In the competition department at the Lincoln Cars HQ, brand-new Anglias are being prepared for the 1961 Monte Carlo Rally. Only one works Zephyr took part in that event: the other Zephyrs here are the 1961 Safari cars, as is possibly the Anglia on the extreme left without roof spotlamp. The works rally cars at this time were painted a distinctive high-visibility yellow.

used to save time wherever possible. (To qualify for international recognition, record-breaking cars may only use spare parts actually carried in the vehicle during the attempt.)

Extensive practising took place during the week before the event, and it was found that the Anglias could not quite manage the lap times necessary at Goodwood to achieve the 10,000 miles in the allotted time. Team Manager Jeff Uren had used Michelin X radial-ply tyres with great success on his racing Zephyr, and as cornering speeds were the problem now, he suggested a departure from standard in respect of tyres by replacing the Anglias' 5.20 x 13 cross-plies with appropriate Michelin X covers. Running at 45psi, the Xs brought the lap times down from around 2 minutes 23 seconds to 2 minutes 15 seconds, this useful saving being sufficient to bring the 10,000-miles target within reach, so the decision was taken to use these tyres. This proved to be particularly wise, as during the event torrential rain

fell for five days, the 3 inches of rainfall recorded being the equivalent to a month's normal average!

For safety's sake, a shoulder harness was fitted to each car, as were twin spotlights to ensure adequate illumination at racing speeds on the Goodwood circuit, which was unlit, although reflectors and some marker lights were installed at the track for the occasion. Identification lamps were also fitted to the cars to aid the timekeepers during darkness. Each car had a radio to relieve the monotony of hours at the wheel, and a Halda Speedpilot, as used in rally cars, informed the driver whether he was ahead of or behind schedule. A Speedwell electronic rev-counter completed the special equipment on board.

Driving car No 1 were Graham Hill, Cuth Harrison and Keith Ballisat; in car No 2 were Bruce McLaren, Edward Harrison and Tom Wisdom; Roy Salvadori, John Mitchell and Gordon Wilkins were in charge of Anglia No 3. Relays were organized so that each driver had three hours on/three hours off, then three hours on, followed by a 12 hour rest period. During their rest periods, Hill, McLaren, Salvadori and Ballisat took flying lessons, having hired a light plane and instructor for the week, the plane being based in the middle of the circuit. The other drivers, however, went off to

play golf. Refuelling took place at the three-hourly intervals, the nearside front tyres were replaced after six hours (the cars were running in a clockwise direction), and all four tyres were replaced after each 12 hours of running time. Pit stops took an average of 90 seconds: no oil changes or greasing were carried out over the entire distance, the engines simply being topped up with BP Visco-Static multigrade oil whenever necessary. The nature of the Goodwood circuit, at the Anglias' level of performance, was such that the brakes were rarely needed, Graham Hill finding that it was just possible to achieve a 60mph lap speed without using the brakes at all.

The endurance test had started on September 26: at 3.30pm on October 3 the three Anglias completed their week-long stint in echelon formation in front of an assembly of guests invited by the Ford Motor Company. However, the test had not been entirely without trouble. Car No 1 had completed 10,468.8 miles (4,362 laps) at an average speed of 62.34mph and a fuel consumption (Shell Premium) of 32.07mpg, but a burnt-out exhaust valve at about half-distance had necessitated attention, and to save time the cylinder-head had been replaced. A similar problem arose on car No 2 at about the same distance and this one, too, had the cylinder head replaced. The nearside front hub bearing was changed twice on this car during the run, at the end of which it had completed 10,432.2 miles (4,343 laps) at 61.89mph and 32.715mpg. These particular troubles did not afflict car No 3, but it was nevertheless the most unfortunate of the trio, being rolled into the ditch at Lavant Corner by Roy Salvadori after only 512 laps. Although the damage was not serious, some panelbeating and a new front suspension strut at one side were necessary before Salvadori — who, thanks to the safety harness, was unhurt — continued his stint. The driving team then made up much of the delay before trouble struck once more when a rear axle halfshaft broke after 9,588 miles had been completed. Another quick repair job saw No 3 back in action again, and at the end it had completed 10,365.6 miles (4,319 laps) to record a 61.53mph average at 31.85mpg, a particularly noteworthy effort by the drivers in view of the delays, alarms and excursions suffered.

116

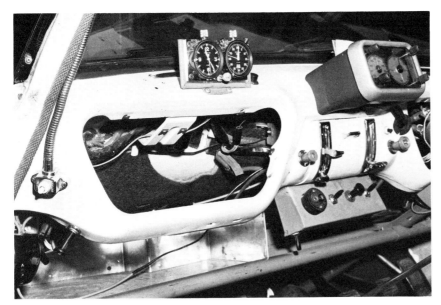

Facia of a works team rally Anglia in preparation. Two stop watches face the navigator, a flexible map lamp runs up the screen pillar, and a centrally-mounted Halda Speed Pilot tells the crew whether they are maintaining the required average speed. A horn button is provided for the navigator and the parcel shelf is divided to stop its contents sliding about.

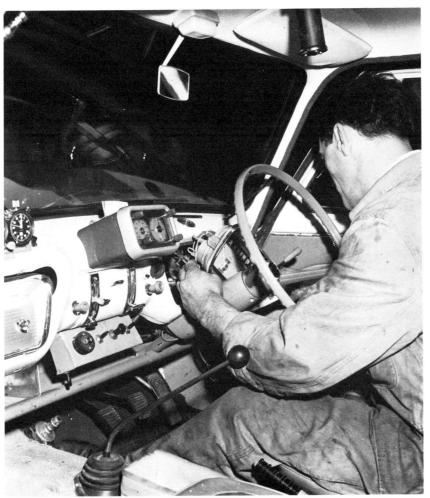

The standard instrument panel was retained and is being refitted here after the installation of the ammeter which can be seen just below the screen. Protruding from the facia near the righthand screen pillar is an additional headlamp flasher, within reach of the driver's hand on the wheel. Projecting from above is the handle of the roof-mounted swivelling spotlamp.

117

Soon after this, another Anglia completed a remarkable long-distance run which had taken place in Europe. Sponsored by Ford Austria, this car left Salzburg on April 14 to motor through every country in Western Europe on a journey which would take it up into Norway and as far south as Sicily. Conditions ranging from 14 degrees Fahrenheit to 105 degrees were encountered, with altitudes up to 9,000ft also involved. Some 208 frontiers were crossed as the Anglia maintained its near 24 hours-a-day schedule over all types of road in the hands of many drivers, including Ford Austria employees and dealers, motoring journalists, members of the public and, finally, racing driver Stirling Moss. Four people were normally carried, including a non-driving observer at all times, and when Moss drove the Anglia into the Vienna Sports Stadium on October 30 it had completed 75,000 miles during which it had averaged 36mpg.

In November, Anne Hall added a second Ladies Cup to her credit in the new Anglia by repeating her previous year's performance in the RAC Rally, bringing the car in just ahead of Pat Moss' Austin-Healey Sprite and Ewy Rosqvist's Volvo. The Anglias had just failed, however, to win the up-to-1,000cc category, Anne Hall's car being behind Phil Crabtree's Anglia and Tiny Lewis' class-winning Triumph Herald. Two months later, January 1961, saw Anne Hall realize one of her most cherished ambitions when she won the Ladies Cup at Monte Carlo after a trouble-free run in the Anglia.

The classifications for the East African Safari in 1961 were altered slightly, and that year's Anglia team found themselves in the 851-to-1,300cc class, in which they were involved in a straight fight with a strong

The studded spare tyre suggests preparation for a winter event, probably the Monte. In international events, Anglias often competed under the regulations for Group 2 (Improved Series Production Touring Cars), which permitted only limited modifications. An Anglia for this category would be fitted with a larger, 24mm-choke carburettor with bigger jets, and a raised compression ratio cylinder head. As acceleration was more important than a high cruising speed, the 4.444:1 axle ratio would be used.

Monte Carlo Rally 1962: veteran competitor Tom Wisdom, who had contested the 1939 Monte in a Ford 8hp Model 7Y, leans nonchalantly on the Anglia whilst partner Jeff Uren attends to something inside the car.

Volkswagen entry. Unlike the previous year, when rain had resulted in deep mud, a prolonged drought now meant extremely dusty conditions with the added problem of wild animals roaming along the roadsides in search of what grass remained in the verges. Only 8 miles out of Nairobi, the first casualty in the rally was a Fiat 2100, which went out after colliding heavily with a zebra. Two tight sections just after entering Tanganyika resulted in penalties for many cars, and the first of the Volkswagens went out with a broken crankcase sustained on the rocky road. By Dar es Salaam 17 cars were out, and when the survivors reached Nairobi at the end of the 2,000-miles southern loop only one of the Volkswagens remained. The Anglia of Peter Hughes was leading the 1,300cc class, and was in fifth place overall, with the similar cars of Mike Sutcliffe and Jeff Uren still going strong, but behind the remaining Volkswagen and a Peugeot 403 in the same class. Only 49 of the 77 starters were fit to tackle the 1,300-miles northern loop, and as this part of the rally featured some tarmac sections early on, the fast cars — Mercedes 220s, Zephyrs, a Humber Super Snipe and the bigger Peugeots — forged ahead, leaving the Hughes Anglia back in 10th place. The remaining Volkswagen was effectively out of the running when it left the route at Nanyuki in order to have a new gearbox fitted, gearbox troubles, including broken mountings due to the high-speed travel over rocky, unmade tracks, proving to be the major cause eliminating the

'I loved the Anglia, you could really fling it about', said Anne Hall recently: here she shows how at Monte Carlo in 1962.

Volkswagens this time. Meanwhile, in the mountainous section near Meru, the Peugeot 403 of Jennings and Partridge had lost time after overturning, and the Anglias were now holding the first three places in the class.

The Anglias of Hughes and Sutcliffe kept going well, but Jeff Uren's car was giving some trouble. Gear selection was becoming a problem, reverse gear now being unobtainable, and there was a heart-stopping moment when, on a rough, unmade section, the Anglia left the road and headed for the bush with Jeff fighting furiously to slew the car round so it would at least end up facing the road. It did, and was soon extricated and back on course, following the other two Anglias into the finish for another first, second and third in the small-car class in the world's toughest rally.

No further major honours came to the Anglia during 1961, although a privately entered export Anglia did remarkably well in the tough 3,500-miles Liège-Sofia-Liège, which took the competitors through the worst conditions possible in northern Italy, Bulgaria and Yugoslavia. Out of 85

At the wheel of a very different Anglia, Anne Hall tries her skill on a brake reaction tester at a road safety exhibition. If this had been the Monte, it's unlikely that the policeman would have had time to smile – when Anne was doing it for real it was no laughing matter!

starters, only eight finished, including the lone Anglia which was the only under-1,500cc-engined car to complete the course.

1962 saw the Anglias in action in many of the major rallies, and although no awards were gained at Monte Carlo, the Safari provided yet another class win. Ford concentrated its Safari entry this year on the new Mk3 Zodiac (which came 1st and 2nd in its class), but a sudden change in the weather conditions during the southern loop, run as the second stage this time, adversly affected the big-car classes, which left Nairobi later than the small cars. The small cars got through the already muddy Mbulu escarpment section without too much trouble, but just as the first of the bigger cars arrived, the heavens opened. Torrential rain saw the large cars wallowing in deep mud, and the leading Mercedes, Rover 3 litres, Zodiacs and Fiat 2300s were soon out of the running for outright victory. Up ahead, Mike Armstrong, who had co-driven with Jeff Uren the previous two years, was battling well with his Anglia, as was Peter Hughes. However, this year Volkswagen got some revenge, with the Fjasted/Schmider car taking

The Anglia was popular with the clubmen too: a privately-entered example gets away from a checkpoint on the 1962 RAC Rally.

outright victory: the best of the Anglias was Armstrong's car in 4th place overall. The Anglias, though, had taken first and second place ahead of the Auto Union 1000s in the 851-to-1,000cc class.

In May, Anne Hall did well to win the up-to-1,000cc class in the Greek Acropolis Rally, a 2,500-miles event of which much was over unpaved roads. Two privately-entered Anglias finished the Liège-Sofia-Liège in August, the Charlier/Mosbeux car winning the 850-to-1,000cc class. This performance was a repeat of the previous year's success, as the two Anglias this year were the only finishers with engines of under 1,500cc, some 40 cars in this category having failed to reach the end.

The newly announced Anglia Super 1200 was the basis of the Ford

1962 RAC Rally again: an Anglia on a forest track, terrain increasingly familiar on this event from the 1960s onwards.

works entry in the 1962 RAC Rally, a three-car team being entered along with a lone Cortina, making that model's international rallying debut in the hands of Jeff Uren. Entered in the up-to-1,600cc sports car/tuned touring car category, the 1,198cc Anglias had engine modifications which included Cosworth cylinder heads, and were reputed to be genuine 100mph cars. Disc brakes at the front were employed. The principal opposition in this class came from the BMC works Mini-Coopers, and at the end the Aaltonen/Ambrose Mini-Cooper took the class win from Henry Taylor's Anglia by a margin of just 2 penalty points, the BMC car having incurred 352 penalties against the Anglia's 354. These two cars were fifth and sixth overall in an event won for the third year in succession by the remarkable Erik Carlsson/Saab combination.

The most impressive Anglia display in 1962 was without doubt that provided by a lone car which, as a private venture, embarked upon a record-breaking spree at the fast, banked Montlhéry circuit near Paris in October. Six enthusiasts — Peter Doughty, Michael and Tony Brookes,

Arthur Taylor, John Clarke and Gerry Boxall — decided on an attempt to break the International Class G speed and endurance records for production cars up to 1,000cc, these records dating back to 1957 when a cleaned-up Austin A35 had lapped Montlhéry for a week at 74mph. A new Anglia was ordered, with export suspension, laminated windscreen and a heater. The £13 Performance Plus Ford tuning kit was also fitted, and the car went to tuning expert Don Moore, at Cambridge, for careful setting up. The engine was stripped and the crankshaft balanced before reassembly, whilst cylinder head work was confined to polishing the combustion chambers and ports. As there would be no need to ease the throttle at all on the banked circuit, Moore wisely set up the carburation appreciably richer than would normally be the case, avoiding the possibility of burning out the valves or holing the pistons due to a lean mixture during flat-out driving. The propeller shaft was balanced, and bearing in mind that some previous record-breaking attempts at Montlhéry had resulted in cars sustaining broken leaf springs on the circuit's rather rough and patchy surface, the

Another privately-entered Anglia, this time a left-hand-drive car on foreign registration plates – 1963 Monte Carlo Rally again.

1963 East African Safari Rally: Peter Hughes swings his Anglia 1200 into a hairpin bend.

123

1963 East African Safari Rally: the Hughes/Young Anglia makes good time on one of the smoother sections.

1963 East African Safari Rally: the Hughes/Young car on the Mount Elgon stage. The footrests on the bumper and grab handles on the boot lid are to enable the co-driver to ride on the rear of the car to improve traction through deep mud.

They made it! Peter Hughes and Bill Young look overjoyed at the finish of the 1963 Safari, having brought their Anglia home in 2nd place overall in an event in which only seven cars finished out of 84 starters.

An Anglia on its way to victory in the 1966 Canadian Winter Rally. The 105E had an excellent record on this two-day, 1,200-miles event, winning it outright in 1961, 1962 and 1966, and winning the team prize in 1960, 1961, 1964 and 1966.

Anglia's rear springs were coated in graphited grease and then bound very tightly with tape. An additional 10-gallon fuel tank was installed in the boot from where it fed the car's original tank, and quick refuelling was guaranteed via a $3\frac{1}{2}$-inch diameter filler neck in the boot lid.

Two spotlamps were fitted, but the bumpers, grille and other front-end embellishments were removed, and all gaps around the head and side lamps, windscreen pillars, etc, were filled and smoothed out with Plasticine. This aerodynamic treatment was reckoned to compensate for the drag of the spotlamps and go some way towards making up for the weight of the small items of spares and the toolkit carried in the car, as this was of course an official record attempt. The 5.25 Dunlop D9 tyres raised the gearing very slightly, thus completing the 'speed' modifications, whilst inside was a seat belt and additional instrumentation consisting of a rev-counter, an oil pressure gauge and an ammeter.

The Ford Motor Company sent competition department mechanic Jack Welch along to give advice and assistance if necessary, and at 2pm on Wednesday October 24 the Anglia began its attempt. Pit stops were scheduled for every three hours, at which 12 gallons of Total petrol were taken on whilst a change of drivers took place. A pint of Castrol XL was also needed at each stop, as the engine was emptying this amount out of the crancase breather tube during the three-hour flat-out stints. As long as the temperature gauge read normal the radiator was left unchecked, as this would have added 15 seconds or so to the stops, which were averaging around 58 seconds. During the Saturday, the exhaust system broke away from the manifold joint under the bonnet, with the immediate result that, apart from the increase in noise, lap times improved by more than a second as the Anglia pulled another 200 revs (5,400rpm) along the straights. Nevertheless, the car was brought in to have this fault attended to, and the pipe was wired to the manifold during a stop, which cost $9\frac{1}{2}$ minutes in all. No further troubles were encountered, and it was not until the Monday afternoon, after the 5-day record had been broken, that it was decided to give the car a slightly more thorough check during a $4\frac{1}{2}$-minute stop. All four wheels and tyres were replaced, the fronts having been replaced once earlier on, and the radiator was now checked for the only time — it needed a pint. One spark plug was checked, and as this was alright it was replaced and the others left well alone.

The run continued troublefree, and on Wednesday afternoon Ford Competition Manager, Syd Henson, walked out on to the edge of the circuit with the chequered flag as the Anglia completed its week-long ordeal. The fastest lap, 64.8 seconds, had equalled 88mph, but wind, rain and some fog had sometimes pulled the speed down, the slowest lap times, in fog, being 90 seconds. Nevertheless, 14,010.59 miles had been covered at an average speed of 83.4mph; six new records had been set — those for 15,000km, 20,000km, four, five, six and seven days — everything, in fact, that the team had set out to achieve.

Two Anglias were amongst the works Ford entries for the 1963 Monte, a 1200 Super and a fully modified 997cc car fitted with a Formula Junior engine, front disc brakes and a long-range fuel tank. These two cars were teamed with a Cortina, the other works team entry being three Mk3 Zodiacs. In the event, however, it was the private entries which were best placed, Sydney Allard and his son, Alan, taking first and second places respectively, in the up-to-1,000cc modified category in their supercharged Allardettes.

A strong Cortina entry figured in the East African Safari in April, with the Anglia's position in the works team now definitely under threat from the newer car. Nevertheless, past class-winner and local driver Peter Hughes was in the event once again with an Anglia, this time a 1200 Super.

The 84 cars left Nairobi and headed for Kampala, as the northern loop was being tackled first once again. No-one remained unpenalized for long, but after the first special stage, a steep unmade track climbing from around 5,000ft to almost 9,000ft at Mau Marok, Erik Carlsson, although penalized, established a good lead in his Saab. After this, the rains came again, as in the previous year, leaving all roads into Uganda inches deep in mud, with the result that record penalties were incurred for this section by the time the runners reached Kampala. Carlsson was still in front, with the highest placed Ford, a Zodiac, in seventh place, and Hughes' Anglia ninth. After leaving Kampala, slippery red mud on the roads around Mount Elgon

Saloon-car racing entertainment: a Super Speed Anglia in action at Oulton Park, closely pursued by a pack of Mini-Coopers.

saw many of the big cars bogged down, and although Carlsson still led the way, the Fords started moving up, with the Anglia in second place ahead of three GT Cortinas. A bout of misfiring, however, caused Hughes to slow, and at Nairobi the Anglia was back in third place. Carlsson was still in front, followed by four Fords, then a Mercedes 190 and another Cortina GT in seventh place.

On the southern loop many more were soon dropping out, and at Dar es Salaam only 28 cars remained, Carlsson leading from Younghusband's Cortina, then the Anglia with Nowicki's Peugeot 404 close behind. Soon after leaving Dar, Carlsson went out as the Saab's front suspension finally succumbed to the East African terrain, and the Cortina GT enjoyed a brief spell in front before it too failed with a holed sump. By this time the Peugeot had overtaken Hughes, so the Anglia was lying second yet again, but being hard-pressed by Cardwell's Mercedes 220 in third place. Nevertheless, the game Anglia held on to the end where only three minutes separated it from the big Mercedes at the finish of what had been the toughest Safari yet, with only seven cars clocking in at Nairobi.

Although the Anglia's career as a front-line rally car was now over, it had yet to reach its greatest heights in the sphere of saloon car racing. Ever since its introduction, the 105E had been popular with drivers and spectators, particularly so in those events where regulations permitted extensive modifications which could turn small cars into giant-killers. Anglias successful at this level were, of course, almost inevitably quite far removed from the willing little saloon which took the family on seaside trips: one such car was that raced by Doc Merfield (an oral surgeon) in the early 1960s. Prepared by Willment, Merfield's Anglia had a 1,475cc engine, the basis of which was a Classic 109E unit suitably over-bored. A mildly reworked cylinder head, twin Weber carburettors, a four-branch exhaust manifold feeding into an expansion box and megaphone tail-pipe, and a Willment camshaft were sufficient to produce 125bhp at 7,300rpm. Bottom-end strengthening of the unit was confined to new main-bearing caps machined from the solid, whilst the standard crankshaft and connect-rods were balanced and polished. A five-speed gearbox with Hewland internals in the standard Ford casing was employed, the four upper ratios giving approximately 60, 75, 90 and 105mph at 7,000rpm. Disc brakes were fitted at the front, where the standard MacPherson struts were retained, but embraced by cut-down Mk2 Zephyr coil springs. An additional anti-roll bar was also used. Flattened leaf springs lowered the rear end slightly, Koni dampers replacing the originals, and Dunlop racing tyres on the Ford rims were considered to be quite sufficient.

This was, of course, a serious racing machine, and although the Anglia's lines remained unaltered — no flared arches, etc — the car was virtually devoid of interior trim, with a single padded seat welded and bolted to the uncarpeted floor. Perspex side and rear windows, and alloy doors and boot lid were further departures from standard. The modifications endowed this Anglia with enough performance to hold off cars such as 3.8-litre Mk2 Jaguars on occasion. The car was tested by *The Motor*, for whom it recorded a 0 to 90mph time of 18.9 seconds, despite a somewhat leisurely take-off (0-30 in 6.9 seconds) due to a high first gear and a desire not to overstress the standard crownwheel and pinion. The maximum speed proved to be 113mph.

Not quite so startling as Doc Merfield's car, but nevertheless very potent, was the Allardette raced by Alan Allard in 1963. This car was also virtually gutted inside, and from a mechanical point of view consisted principally of

The Team Broadspeed Anglias had a remarkably standard external appearance which belied the fact that they were highly-developed racers, their power units, although still of only 997cc, producing over 100bhp, with the aid of down-draught Weber carburettors, for the 1966 season, the year in which John Fitzpatrick won the Saloon Car Championship. The two team cars are shown here during a test session: number 71 was Fitzpatrick's mount.

the Cortina 1500GT engine and drive train, but with the important addition of a Shorrock supercharger, with which it developed 118bhp at 6,500rpm. This specification enabled it to accelerate from rest to 60 and 70mph in 10.5 and 17.1 seconds when it, too, was sampled by *The Motor*, the maximum speed on the 3.9:1 axle and oversize Dunlop racing tyres being estimated at 115mph.

Amongst the other Anglia drivers regularly entertaining the crowds during the 1960s were Chris Craft, Boley Pittard (who had an excellent season in 1964, winning all bar one of the Spring Grove Championship series of races), Mike and John Young in their Superspeed Anglias, Norman Abbot, David Garrat, Brian Peacock and Rod Mansfield, who campaigned as Team Anglia with a 1,600cc Cosworth Lotus-engined car and another with a five-bearing pushrod engine bored out to 1,650cc. Nick Brittan had his Anglia 'Green Bean', and Anita Taylor and John Fitzpatrick were seen in the highly developed Broadspeed Anglias. In 1966 John Fitzpatrick won the Saloon Car Championship outright in one of the Broadspeed cars, a particularly meritorious win in view of the fact that

Anglias in the 1980s: Frank Collins at the wheel of the much-modified car in which he and his son, Martin, compete in sprint events.

these Anglias retained the 997cc engine (albeit in extremely highly-tuned form) which, of course, powered the vast majority of everyday Anglias. In fact, the Group 5 regulations under which the Broadspeed team cars were competing, whilst allowing considerable tuning, stipulated that the cars must weigh at least 97% of the catalogued weight: therefore, the Broadspeed cars also looked remarkably standard as little could be removed for weight-saving purposes. Inside, too, much of the original trim was retained, just the driver's seat being changed for one of the racing variety. There the close similarities ended, though, as Ralph Broad had managed to extract more than a 100bhp from the 1-litre unit, and this was transmitted to the rear axle via a non-synchromesh Hewland five-speed gearbox. A limited-slip differential was fitted, and rear axle ratios varied according to the circuit. Disc brakes at the front were fitted as usual on competition Anglias, as was an additional anti-roll bar clamped to the original. At the rear, too, was an anti-roll bar, and the normal leaf springs had given way to coils, with the axle located by radius arms. For 1967, Tecalemit Jackson fuel-injection replaced the Webers on the Broadspeed cars, and the 997cc engine now produced an astonishing 124bhp at 9,200rpm – more than three times the output of the standard unit.

Anglias in the 1980s: the road-going Anglia which is campaigned in Classic Saloon races by Tom Luff.

Nevertheless, the Anglia just failed to take the championship that year, Fitzpatrick finishing runner-up to Frank Gardner's 4.7-litre Ford Falcon, and just ahead of John Rhodes' Mini-Cooper S. The coming of the Escort, of course, demoted the Anglia somewhat, although the distinctive 105E shape could be seen in action for some years in the hands of the relatively low-budget private entrants.

Today, Anglias can again be seen in action regularly in the very popular Pre '65 Classic Saloon races, as well as Historic rallies, sprints, hillclimbs and so on, with cars ranging from the mildly tuned to the fully reworked and very formidable. Tom Luff regularly competes in Class D (1,000cc) in Pre '65 races with his road-legal and remarkably standard-looking 997cc

Archie Inglis uses every inch of the track at Scammonden hill climb in July 1984. For road use the alloy wheels and Pirelli P7s seen here are replaced by steel wheels and more-normal profile tyres, with which the car looks more like a collector's car than a highly-developed competition machine.

Anglia. This car was raced in the late 1960s and early 1970s by Bev Steed, after which it lay idle for 10 years or so before Tom Luff acquired it in 1982 and immediately undertook an extensive rebuild. The engine has now been prepared by Uptune Racing, who had considerable experience with the Anglia unit in their Formula 3 cars of that era, and the gearbox is the Ford 2000E close-ratio unit. At the front are Classic struts and disc brakes, whilst a Watts linkage helps locate the back axle.

Another Anglia which saw competitive action in its early days, and has happily survived to compete again, is the ex-Alan Peer East Anglian Championship-winning car of 1967. Purchased by Frank Collins in 1971, and raced successfully by him until badly damaged at Silverstone some time later, this car was extensively rebuilt in 1983. Since then it has been used in sprint events by Frank and his son Martin, in whose hands it won an event at North Weald aerodrome in 1983, narrowly beating a 1,760cc Escort. Differing considerably from standard, this Anglia features a one-

Twin Webers are a snug fit in the engine compartment of Archie Inglis' Anglia. The battery has vacated its usual position in the offside front corner and now resides in the boot, where it helps to balance the weight distribution.

piece fibreglass front end, alloy doors, boot lid and boot floor, and Perspex side and rear windows. The power train consists of a Cosworth-tuned Lotus Ford twin-cam 1,558cc unit with twin Webers, a 2000E gearbox and a locked (welded-up) Lotus Cortina differential. Lotus suspension units, a double anti-roll bar and disc brakes are used at the front, with another anti-roll bar being a feature of the lowered rear end. The rear brake drums have also been lightened. Unfortunately, a broken cam bucket sustained during a practice session necessitated cylinder head removal, and the car missed much of the 1984 season as a result.

Since being built to rally specification during 1979/80, the very much-modified Anglia of Simon Bridge has enjoyed considerable success, finishing runner-up in the 1983 West Midland Road Rally Championship and proving itself capable of outright victory in individual events. The power for this extremely potent machine comes from a 1,700cc engine built by Tyler Racing Engines, and based on the five-bearing block bored out to 83.5mm. A big-valve cylinder head (Cosworth valves and springs), twin Dellorto 40 DHLA carburettors, a Lumenition ignition system with Escort Twin-cam distributor, Aldon Hot Rod big-bore four-into-one

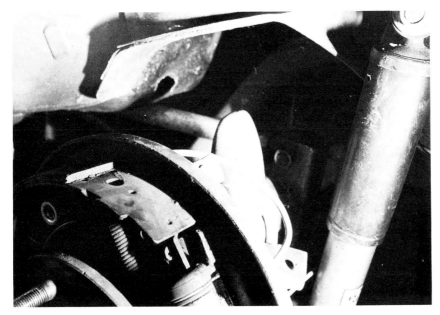

Rear suspension details of 6675 RE, the Archie Inglis car. The radius arm can be seen going forward through the bulkhead to locate on the crossmember under the rear seats.

exhaust manifold and Aldon RS2000 exhaust system all contribute to a massive 160bhp at the flywheel. Lightened and balanced connecting rods, a tuftrided crankshaft and Cosworth big-end bolts are bottom-end features, and lubrication is attended to by a high-pressure oil pump, large capacity filter, oil cooler and a fully baffled 10-pint sump. An alloy competition bellhousing, 2000E gearbox and Anglia 1200 propeller shaft take the power to a 4.1:1 Salisbury limited-slip diff, from where it reaches the rear wheels via Escort Twin-cam halfshafts. The front suspension in this case is by Corsair struts, with Mk1 Cortina top mounts and the usual double anti-roll bars, whilst at the rear are uprated Anglia springs, Bilstein turreted shock absorbers, twin radius arms and a Panhard rod. Disc brakes on all four wheels are employed to tame the beast, those at the front being made up of Cortina Mk3 and Mk4 components, with Capri 3-litre pads, whilst at the rear are specially adapted Chrysler 180 discs and calipers. The system is dual-circuit, and employs two Girling Powerstop servo units. The dual-circuit master cylinder is the Bedford CF unit, and a Mini restrictor valve gives the correct front/rear bias. Rack-and-pinion steering gear, utilizing Escort and Mk3 Cortina parts with a Morris Minor 1000 rack, completes the running gear.

Built specially for hillclimb events is the immaculate 1959 Anglia which made its competition debut in 1984 in the hands of Archie Inglis. With its original, unchanged all-steel bodywork, complete with grille, bumpers, etc. this maroon-painted car looks like a well-kept collectors' item: indeed, Archie's intention was to produce a competition machine which could nevertheless be useful whenever necessary as a practical road-going car. Under the bonnet is a five-bearing engine which started life as an Escort 1300 unit, but which now has a capacity of 1,428cc as a result of being bored-out to 85mm. Powermax flat-top pistons are used, and the standard 1300 crankshaft has been balanced and tuftrided. A pre-crossflow cylinder head is employed, giving a compression ratio of 10.5:1 and with valve gear consisting of Burton steel posts and rocker shaft, whilst a Kent A6-profile camshaft looks after the valve timing. Two 40 DCOE Webers supply the mixture, and a Jeff Howe manifold and exhaust system get the gases away. Approximately 90bhp is provided at the rear wheels, having arrived there via standard transmission including, during the 1984 season, the Anglia's original 4.125:1 axle, although a 4.444:1 ratio and a limited-slip differential were used for 1985.

The seemingly almost inevitable Classic front strut/disc brake set-up is employed, along with the usual additional anti-roll bar, and at the rear are flattened Anglia van springs complete with an extra leaf. Spax shock absorbers and twin radius rods complete the suspension arrangements here. Rose-jointed to the rear axle, the radius rods go through holes cut into the rear bulkhead to locate in bushed mountings on the cross-member under the rear seats. Escort Twin-cam rear brakes are used, there is no servo, and as the car is normally facing uphill when being driven in anger, standard pad and lining material is quite sufficient.

So almost 20 years after its production demise the versatile Anglia can still be seen giving a good account of itself amongst its contemporaries and sometimes much more modern machinery, and looks all set to continue to do so, whether in circuit racing, sprinting, rallying, or hillclimbing.

CHAPTER 8

An Anglia in the 1980s

Purchase and ownership

For today's enthusiast looking for a small economical car with collectable status, there will almost certainly be something from the long-running Anglia/Prefect/Popular series which fits the bill. Very collectable indeed now are the 'upright' models, and whilst a casual appraisal of these may suggest a certain lack of practicality for use as everyday cars, this is not necessarily always the case. In terms of performance, the 8hp cars particularly are out of their depth, so to speak, amongst present-day traffic, but if this factor is accepted at the outset and the car driven accordingly, with due respect for other road users, then this little Ford can still give a lot of pleasure whilst being just as useful in most other respects as the more powerful 10hp Prefects and Populars.

Roomy bodywork, with sensible headroom and almost unbelievably good access are excellent features of this range by comparison with today's small cars, although the situation is, of course, reversed when it comes to comparing riding comfort, for whilst the seats are quite good in these old cars, the Model T-inspired springing system simply cannot compare with the sophisticated suspension set-ups employed today. Handling qualities, too, inevitably fall far short of modern standards, and not just because of the antiquated suspension, but also because the slightly tail-heavy weight distribution of these Fords produces a lack of directional stability which results in the driver becoming rather hard-worked if brisk averages are to be maintained. While the flexible nature of these engines, particularly the 10hp unit, does enable reasonably good progress to be made if the roads are clear, the lack of an intermediate ratio between second and top gear severely limits the overtaking abilities in today's often heavy traffic conditions.

If long-distance journey times are planned around these limitations, which, of course, do not really matter on local trips, shopping and so on, there is little else to be said against making these admittedly old-fashioned Fords work for their keep once again. Certainly, over an extended mileage, an example which is well-preserved or has perhaps been extensively restored to really good all-round order, should prove not only a very dependable, but also an extremely economical proposition indeed. These are rugged cars, and with servicing carried out approximately in line with the manufacturer's original recommendations they are quite capable of running considerable mileages without much need for replacement of

parts. One respect where modern developments have helped is in lubrication, and a newly reconditioned engine which is lubricated with a good-quality multigrade oil, with oil and filter changes around the 5,000-miles intervals, should have a significantly longer life potential than the original units of this type 30 or 35 years ago.

As when purchasing any used car, the buyer should know beforehand just what the model's weak points are, and when considering the 'upright' Fords a check should certainly be made on the condition of the separate chassis-frame where its longitudinal members sweep upwards to clear the rear axle. At this point, mud can accumulate in the channel-section members and cause corrosion to set in; elsewhere, however, this chassis is not prone to serious deterioration. The bodywork should, of course, be examined carefully, particularly at its mounting points, and along where the running-boards join the sill area on those cars so equipped. Deterioration in the bodywork of these cars is usually easy to spot, as, unlike many monocoques, these are not full of hidden mud and water traps, and even an inexperienced buyer who takes time and care over the examination should be able to come to a reasonably accurate assessment of its condition.

If the car under scrutiny is one of the last of the line, the 103E Popular, and it obviously requires plenty of attention to the bodywork, it will perhaps be better to leave it alone anyway. Plenty of these have survived, and a better example, quite realistically priced, will almost certainly be found within a reasonable time if the search continues with diligence. The earlier Anglias and Prefects are rather more difficult to find, and as a result are perhaps more collectable than the subsequent Popular. Their higher trim level and, in the Prefect's case, the convenience of four doors also adds somewhat to their desirability, and if one of these is particularly being sought a harder search and almost certainly a higher purchase price will be involved than for a Popular, always bearing in mind, of course, the overall condition of the car.

When checking out the mechanical elements of these particular Fords it is essential that those with no past experience of the model realize that despite being in production in Popular guise until 1959, these are 1930s

136

cars. Thus, mechanical refinement, noise levels, etc, will not compare with more up-to-date machinary in the small-car class. From the engine, expect some blue smoke in the exhaust if it is a well-used unit; these engines always have a tendency to burn some oil, even when in good condition. When pulling hard there may be some evidence inside the car of engine fumes, this being another characteristic of the unit long before it reaches a worn-out condition. During the 1950s, hose and pipe devices were available from accessory makers which could be attached to the oil filler/breather tube and which fed the fumes into the carburettor intake, or alternately down the side of the engine and out underneath the car. It should not be too difficult for an owner to devise something similar today.

Acceleration in first and second gears should feel quite sufficient for a good getaway, but the gap between second and top will be noticed, although the engine pulls very well all the way from below 20mph to 55mph or so on top gear. The direct-acting gearchange should be accurate and very quick, but unless the gearbox is a recently reconditioned unit, second gear may well jump out of engagement on the overrun, this being a common fault on these models which was often accepted as quite normal by their owners. If in well maintained condition the brakes will feel reasonably powerful, and whilst the usual inspection of the steering gear should be carried out it must be remembered that the indifferent directional stability of the model is characteristic and not necessarily indicative of any serious wear in the running gear. Suitable tyres are still available from either Avon or Lambrook Tyres, whilst owners of these Fords in recent years have also found the imported Mabor General tyre from Portugal to be entirely satisfactory.

Once a purchase has been made, membership of the Ford Sidevalve Owners' Club is not just desirable, it is almost essential. In existence now for 15 years, this club has enormous experience of the day-to-day running and maintenance of these cars, and offers an excellent service to the owners in respect of spare parts, including many remanufactured items which would otherwise be unobtainable. Bearing in mind that the chassis from many of these Fords ended their days clothed in glass-fibre or alloy bodies as Ford Specials, often with highly tuned engines, and that the tuning equipment such as alloy cylinder heads and twin carburettor installations sometimes appears for sale secondhand, the club offers a Panhard rod axle locating system which enables the beam-axle Ford to handle a reasonable performance increase, this modification perhaps also being desirable for its increased stability alone on an untuned car. Overall, with a little foresight, for example stocking certain service items at home, the Sidevalve Club member should have no problems in running an 'upright' Ford as a dependable form of everyday transport.

Also well catered-for by the Ford Sidevalve Owners' Club are the 100E models, with which rather different considerations have to be borne in mind when assessing an example of the range with a view to purchase. The monocoque bodyshell, whilst extremely robust when in good condition, can nevertheless suffer from serious corrosion in certain vital areas, apart from the usual rusting which does little more than mar the appearance. Very carefully checked underneath should be the chassis-type outriggers, the inner sill areas and the rear spring attachment points on the longitudinal members. Whilst deterioration in these areas may well be repairable, the cost of repairs, according to how serious the damage is, may not be cheap, and the price of the car therefore should reflect this. At the front, check also the condition of the front suspension upper mounting points which, although substantially reinforced, can also eventually be dangerously weakened by rust. Repair sections are available, however, to rectify this, as are new outer sills and front wing lower repair sections, which can very effectively tidy-up the exterior at reasonable cost. The rear wheelarch outer lipped section can be repaired by adapting the remarkably similar rear wing outer section of the MG Midget MkII/Sprite MkIII, whilst aft of the arch the 100E's curved lower rear wing is matched closely in curvature by that of the Ford Transit van which, with some surgery of course, can be adapted for repairs.

Mechanically, the 100E has few weak points, although like the earlier sidevalve engines this one, too, can sometimes use more oil than would a modern unit in similar condition. In general, though, this engine is appreciably more refined than that of the original 10hp cars. The hydraulic clutch has a more modern feel to it, and the gearbox has not quite the same reputation as the earlier one for jumping out of second gear. The front suspension and steering gear are really quite modern, and as steering joints, etc, are readily available a 100E should present no insurmountable problems here. The bearing in the MacPherson strut upper mounting can wear out eventually; the bearings are available, but as fitting these involves removal of the suspension units the potential cost of this operation should be borne in mind when checking over the car.

On the road, subject to the running gear being in good condition, and within the limits imposed by its rather skinny 5.20 x 13 crossply tyres, the 100E should feel quite modern in its handling qualities, good directional stability being combined with quick and accurate steering response. Rear axle hop will be noticed, however, if the car is driven hard through bumpy corners. Equipping the saloons with the 5.60 x 13 tyres as used on the estate cars can be of some benefit, whilst there is, of course, a wide choice of modern radial tyres available in the appropriate 145 or 155 x 13 sizes which will impart a worthwhile improvement in the car's overall cornering capabilities. The performance which once put the 100E to the fore in the small-car class is now well down the league, with the gap between second and top gear being much more noticeable in today's traffic than in the model's heyday some 30 years ago. Top-gear flexibility, however, is

excellent, and the 100E will thread its way through towns in this ratio at low speeds in a manner quite impossible in today's small cars.

With its modern OHV engine and four-speed gearbox allied to the established and well-trimmed Prefect four-door bodywork, the 107E model is a tempting proposition; but this, of course, was produced over only a short period of time and is now very rare indeed by comparison with the other small Fords.

Much more recent, and built in the greatest numbers, the 105E Anglia is the easiest way for the enthusiast to buy into the small-Ford scene. Nevertheless, the newest of these Anglias are now approaching 20 years of age, and therefore finding one of these for sale today will usually involve far more than simply looking through the used car columns in the local newspaper. The points vulnerable to corrosion on the 105E range are similar to most monocoques, with the sills, the front wings in the vicinity of the headlamps and at their rear edge adjacent to the door pillar, and the door bottoms, often suffering visibly. A check should also be made of the front suspension upper mounting in the inner wing, as although this model tends to fare better than some later Fords in this respect, corrosion here is now a problem with some Anglias. This need not be terminal, however, as repair sections are available. The rear spring hangers, too, should be

Because its enormous success quickly made it such a familiar sight, it is difficult to recapture the striking impression made by the 105E Anglia with its original and unusual styling when it first appeared in 1959. It proved to be a versatile car and won many friends: a good example could still be an attractive proposition.

checked out carefully. Corrosion in the A post around the door attachment points can also be a serious problem with this body, particularly as the very wide door is rather heavy and so imposes considerable stress in this area. As deterioration here is not always easy to rectify, the opinion of someone with an intimate knowledge of the model should be sought if the car under assessment is obviously suffering badly in this respect.

Mechanically, this model earned a very good reputation, and a high-mileage example which has been sensibly serviced in line with the manufacturer's recommendations may well be in a perfectly satisfactory condition and ready to give a further spell of useful service without major attention. These engines generally used very little oil, so blue smoke in this case could indicate considerable wear, as could excessive fuming out of the rocker cover cap or the crankcase breather tube. If in a good state of tune (it's extremely unlikely that any of the early 'flat spot' carburettors are still in use), these engines will operate cleanly, although not very briskly, from low rpm, and remain mechanically very smooth indeed throughout the revolution range. A slight rumble, more likely on a well-worn 1200 than on a 997cc example, could mean at the very least main bearings well past their prime, or serious crankshaft wear. If this is accompanied by the oil pressure warning light remaining on at anything above a slow idling speed, then anticipate an imminent bottom-end overhaul. Whilst checking over the condition of the running gear it is wise to pay particular attention to the rear springs. These have a tendency to flatten out considerably after an extended mileage, and by the time the clearance between the rubber bump stop and the chassis member has been reduced to an inch, replacement springs are necessary.

The performance of a fully fit example should feel pleasantly lively providing that full use is made of the gearbox, and unlike earlier Anglias, this one, whichever of the two axle ratios is fitted, should prove willing to maintain an agreeable 65mph or so motorway cruise, whilst under more give-and-take conditions it should also have a useful overtaking ability using third gear to around 55 or 60mph. The interchangability of engines between this and later Fords using larger-capacity variations of the Kent engine means that considerable performance improvements can be achieved today in the manner of the Allardettes, or the Superspeed cars, for example. Good roadholding qualities are once again limited somewhat by the standard 5.20 x 13 tyres, and the previous comments about the 100E range in this respect apply equally here.

Mechanical and routine service items are still quite widely available for this model from motor factors and accessory outlets, and anything which is not is almost certain to be obtainable through the 105E Owners' Club. Formed as recently as 1981 by John Colyer and Paul Guinness, this club has done much in a short period of time to ensure a successful future for the surviving 105E cars. Having instigated the remanufacture of many parts which were becoming rare, its members now have access to items as diverse as bodywork repair sections, stainless-steel exhaust pipes and front suspension top-mount bearings, and it would certainly appear that membership of the club is a must for the 105E Anglia owner today.

APPENDIX A
Technical specifications

ANGLIA E04A & E494A

Engine: 4-cylinder in-line, side valves. Bore × stroke 56.6mm × 92.5mm, capacity 933cc. Compression ratio 6.3:1. Maximum power 23.4bhp (nett) at 4,000rpm.
Transmission: 3-speed gearbox. Axle ratio 5.5:1. Mph/1,000rpm: 1st 4.05, 2nd 7.05, top 13.8.
Tyres: Cross-ply, 4.50 × 17.
Brakes: Mechanical, 85sq in lining area.
Dimensions: Length 12ft 9in, width 4ft 9in, height 5ft 4½in, wheelbase 7ft 6in, track 3ft 9in.
Weight: 14¾cwt.

PREFECT E93A & E493A

Engine: 4-cylinder in-line, side valves. Bore × stroke 63.5mm × 92.5mm, capacity 1,172cc. Compression ratio 6.16:1. Maximum power 30.1bhp (nett) at 4,000rpm.
Transmission: 3-speed gearbox. Axle ratio 5.5:1. Mph/1,000rpm: 1st 4.39, 2nd 7.65, top 13.5
Tyres: Cross-ply, 5.00 × 16.
Brakes: Mechanical, 85sq in lining area.
Dimensions: Length 13ft, width 4ft 9in, height 5ft 3½in, wheelbase 7ft 10in, track 3ft 9in.
Weight: 16¾cwt.

POPULAR 103E

Engine: 4-cylinder in-line, side valves. Bore × stroke 63.5mm × 92.5mm, capacity 1,172cc. Compression ratio 6.16:1. Maximum power 30.1bhp (nett) at 4,000rpm.
Transmission: 3-speed gearbox. Axle ratio 5.5:1. Mph/1,000rpm: 1st 4.49, 2nd 7.82, top 13.8.
Tyres: Cross-ply 4.50 × 17.
Brakes: Mechanical, 85sq in lining area.
Dimensions: Length 12ft 8in, width 4ft 9in, height 5ft 4½in, wheelbase 7ft 6in, track 3ft 9in.
Weight: 14½cwt.

ANGLIA, PREFECT, POPULAR 100E

Engine: 4-cylinder in-line, side valves. Bore × stroke 63.5mm × 92.5mm, capacity 1,172cc. Compression ratio 7.0:1. Maximum power 36bhp (nett) at 4,500rpm.
Transmission: 3-speed gearbox. Axle ratio 4.429:1. Mph/1,000rpm: 1st 4.34, 2nd 7.94, top 14.8. Lower indirect ratios from January 1955 give 1st 4.03, 2nd 7.37.
Tyres: Cross-ply 5.20 × 13.
Brakes: Hydraulic, 67.2sq in lining area. From January 1955 76.8sq in lining area.
Dimensions: Length 12ft 6in, width 5ft, height 4ft 10½in, wheelbase 7ft 3in, track 4ft front, 3ft 11½in rear.
Weight: 15¼cwt two-door, 15½cwt four-door.

PREFECT 107E

Engine: 4-cylinder in-line, overhead valves. Bore × stroke 80.96mm × 48.41mm, capacity 997cc. Compression ratio 8.9:1. Maximum power 39bhp (nett) at 5,000rpm.
Transmission: 4-speed gearbox. Axle ratio 4.429:1 Mph/1,000rpm: 1st 3.59, 2nd 6.17, 3rd 10.48, top 14.8
Tyres: Cross-ply 5.20 × 13.
Brakes: Hydraulic, 76.8sq in lining area.
Dimensions: Length 12ft 6in, width 5ft, height 4ft 10½in, wheelbase 7ft 3in, track 4ft front, 3ft 11½in rear.
Weight: 15¾cwt.

ANGLIA 105E

Engine: 4-cylinder in-line, overhead valves. Bore × stroke 80.96mm × 48.41mm, capacity 997cc. Compression ratio 8.9:1. Maximum power 39bhp (nett) at 5,000rpm.
Transmission: 4-speed gearbox. With axle ratio 4.125:1, mph/1,000rpm: 1st 3.9, 2nd 6.7, 3rd 11.37, top 16.07. With axle ratio 4.444:1, mph/1,000rpm: 1st 3.6, 2nd 6.2, 3rd 10.5, top 14.7.
Tyres: Cross-ply 5.20 × 13.
Brakes: Hydraulic, 76.8sq in lining area.
Dimensions: Length 12ft 9½in, width 4ft 9in, height 4ft 8½in, wheelbase 7ft 6½in, track 3ft 10½in front, 3ft 10in rear.
Weight: 15cwt.

ANGLIA SUPER/1200 123E

Engine: 4-cylinder in-line, overhead valves. Bore × stroke 80.96mm × 58.17mm, capacity 1,198cc. Compression ratio 8.7:1 (9.1:1 later). Maximum power 48.5bhp (nett) at 4,800rpm (50bhp nett at 4,900rpm later).
Transmission: 4-speed gearbox. Axle ratio 4.125:1. Mph/1,000rpm: 1st 3.9, 2nd 6.7, 3rd 11.37, top 16.07.
Tyres: Cross-ply 5.20 × 13.
Brakes: Hydraulic, 81.7sq in lining area.
Dimensions: Length 12ft 9½in, width 4ft 9in, height 4ft 8½in, wheelbase 7ft 6½in, track 3ft 10½in front, 3ft 10in rear.
Weight: 15cwt.

APPENDIX B
Performance figures

	0-30mph	0-50mph	0-60mph	0-70mph	Maximum speed	
					Mean	Best
Anglia E04A/E494A	9.6sec	38.3sec	—	—	57.2mph	62.9mph
Prefect E93A/E493A	8.4sec	26.9sec	—	—	59.7mph	62.1mph
Popular 103E	8.6sec	24.1sec	—	—	60.3mph	60.8mph
Anglia/Popular 100E	7.0sec	18.5sec	29.4sec	—	70.2mph	72.6mph
Prefect 100E	7.1sec	20.2sec	32.2sec	—	70.7mph	70.9mph
Anglia 100E with Aquaplane head, twin SUs, 4-branch exhaust	5.0sec	11.4sec	22.8sec	—	78.5mph	83.3mph
Anglia 100E with Elva OHIV head, twin Solex	4.6sec	10.8sec	16.6sec	27.2sec	83.3mph	—
Prefect 107E	5.9sec	16.6sec	27.2sec	—	72.9mph	75.9mph
Anglia 105E 4.125 axle	6.6sec	17.8sec	29.4sec	51.5sec	76.8mph	79.0mph
Anglia 105E 4.444 axle	5.3sec	15.6sec	26.2sec	—	73.3mph	77.6mph
Anglia 105E with Ford Performance Plus conversion, 4.444 axle	5.2sec	13.5sec	20.0sec	32.2sec	78.0mph	—
Anglia 105E Wilen Engineering conversion, high-lift camshaft & pump-type Solex, 4.125 axle	6.1sec	14.9sec	21.9sec	43.3sec	81.6mph	83.0mph
Anglia 105E with Shorrock supercharger, 4.125 axle	5.3sec	12.6sec	17.7sec	26.9sec	88.5mph	91.0mph
Anglia 105E with Arden high-compression head, twin SUs, straight-through silencer	5.5sec	14.8sec	23.2sec	32.3sec	80.6mph	87.0mph
Anglia Allardette with 1,340cc Classic 109E engine, 4.125 axle	5.5sec	14.2sec	21.1sec	34.8sec	79.5mph	81.0mph
Anglia Super/1200 123E	5.1sec	13.8sec	21.6sec	34.9sec	81.8mph	84.2mph

APPENDIX C
Production figures

Anglia E04A (October 1939 — October 1948) 48,000
Anglia E494A (October 1948 — October 1953) 100,000
Prefect E93A (October 1938 — January 1949) 92,000
Prefect E493A (December 1948 — October 1953) 192,000
Popular 103E (November 1953 — August 1959) 155,000

Anglia 100E (October 1953 — August 1959) 345,000
Prefect 100E (December 1953 — August 1959) 255,000
Popular 100E (September 1959 — June 1962) 126,000
Prefect 107E (October 1959 — March 1961) 38,000
Escort estate 100E (October 1955 — April 1961) 33,000
Squire estate 100E (October 1955 — September 1959) 17,000

Anglia 105E (October 1959 — November 1967) 954,000 (includes Anglia Super 123E)
Anglia estate 105E (September 1961 — November 1967) 129,000 (includes 1,198cc estate)

APPENDIX D
Owners' clubs

Ford Sidevalve Owners' Club
Membership Secretary: M. J. Crouch, 30 Earls Close, Bishopstoke, Eastleigh, Hampshire, SO5 6HY.

Overseas Contact: Dave Berry, 33 Terry Street, Sydenham, Sydney, NSW 2044, Australia.

Overseas Sidevalve Clubs
The Ford 8 & 10 Car Club Inc.
PO Box 15587, New Lynn 7, Auckland, New Zealand.

Ford 8 & 10 Car Club
Mrs G. L. Crossley, PO Box 676, New Plymouth, New Zealand.

Tvatumfyra Klubben
Kjell Ohrvall, Rabyvagen 2, S-190 70 Fjardhundra, Sweden.

Engelse Ford Club Nederland
Jos Wouters, Postbus 37, 6566 ZG Millingen a/d Rijn, Netherlands.

Ford 105E Owners' Club
Secretary: Mrs B. Smith, 119 Poplar Avenue, Hove, East Sussex.
Spares Secretary: Douglas Rawson-Harris, 38 Egerton Road, Fallowfield, Manchester.

Spares Specialists
Ken Tingey, Ford 50 Spares, 69 Jolliffe Road, Poole, Dorset, BH15 2HA.

Newford Parts Centre, Abbey Mills, Abbey Village, Chorley, Lancashire.